THE SLOW
COOKER
COOKBOOK

THE SLOW COOKER COOKBOOK

Affordable and convenient meals for your family

RYLAND PETERS & SMALL
LONDON • NEW YORK

Designer Paul Stradling
Editor Abi Waters
Editorial Director Julia Charles
Head of Production Patricia Harrington
Creative Director Leslie Harrington

Indexer Vanessa Bird
Recipe Testing and Adaptation
Not Just Food Ltd

First published in 2023 by
Ryland Peters & Small
20–21 Jockey's Fields
London WC1R 4BW
and
341 E 116th St
New York NY 10029

www.rylandpeters.com

Design and commissioned photographs
© Ryland Peters & Small 2023.
Text © Ghillie Basan, Fiona Beckett, Maxine Clark, Ross
Dobson, Ursula Ferrigno, Silvana Franco, Liz Franklin,
Manisha Gambhir Harkins, Tonia George, Brian Glover,
Rachael Anne Hill, Jennifer Joyce, Caroline Marson, Fiona
Smith, Sonia Stevenson, Sunil Vijayakar, Fran Warde,
Laura Washburn, and Ryland Peters & Small 2023.

Recipes in this book were previously published in *Easy
Slow Cooker* in 2018.

ISBN: 978-1-78879-544-9

10 9 8 7 6 5 4 3 2 1

A CIP record for this book is available from the
British Library.
US Library of Congress Cataloging-in-Publication
Data has been applied for.

Printed in China

notes

- Both British (Metric) and American (Imperial plus
US cup) measurements are included in these recipes for
your convenience; however it is important to work with
one set of measurements and not alternate between the
two within a recipe.

- All spoon measurements are level unless otherwise
specified. A teaspoon is 5 ml and a tablespoon is 15 ml.

- Read your slow cooker manual before you begin and
preheat the slow cooker if required according to the
manufacturer's instructions. Because slow cookers vary
slightly from manufacturer to manufacturer, always
check recipe timings with your model's directions for
a recipe using the same ingredients.

- Where a recipe is finished off under the grill/broiler,
hold the dish with kitchen cloths to remove it from the
machine.

FSC
www.fsc.org
MIX
Paper | Supporting
responsible forestry
FSC® C008047

contents

slow cooker know-how

Slow cookers are electrical appliances with a metal outer sleeve containing an element and a ceramic cooking pot, which sits on top of the element with a lid. (They are often referred to as Crock Pots as a generic name, as this is one of the most widely used brands in the USA.) They cook food at relatively low temperatures compared to other popular cooking methods and are very energy-efficient, using up to 80 per cent less energy than conventional ovens. Slow cookers are useful for busy lifestyles – with as little as 15–20 minutes' preparation time, they can be set up to cook a meal ready for the evening and left on safely while you are out. Slow cookers are designed for moist-heat cooking where moisture in the food condenses on the lid and drops back into the pot, making it a great cooking method for soups and casseroles. In addition, the slow-cooking process can make cheaper cuts of meat tender by cooking them over low heat for several hours, a boon for any cook managing a household budget.

choosing which slow cooker to buy

You can buy around four different sizes of slow cooker, the total capacity and working capacity of which will be printed on the packaging. The working capacity means the maximum space for food.

• **For two people**, go for a mini cooker with a total capacity of 1.5 litres/quarts, of which the working capacity is 1 litres/quart.

• **For four people**, pick a cooker with a total capacity of 3–5 litres/quarts, giving you a working capacity of 2.5 litres/quarts.

- **For six people**, choose a 5-litre/-quart capacity cooker, with a working capacity of 4 litres/quarts.

- **For six to eight people**, look for a 6.5-litre/-quart capacity cooker, with a working capacity of 4.5 litres/quarts.

- **For an average family**, the four person capacity cooker should suit well. Only choose the very large model if you intend on making extra to freeze regularly or you have many mouths to feed. In all sizes, you will find round or oval cookers. The oval is most versatile and best for a baking dish, whole chicken or a joint of meat.

caring for a slow cooker

After cooking in your slow cooker, make sure it is completely cool before attempting to clean it. Unplug it from the mains and remove the ceramic pot (this will be removable in most makes of slow cooker). Wipe the base unit with a warm, damp cloth and dry with a kitchen cloth or paper towels. Be mindful of the fact that the cooker has an electrical plug and lead, which should be kept dry at all times.

Wash the ceramic pot and lid in warm soapy water, making sure to remove any pieces of food from the vent in the lid and around the edges. Soaking is an effective way to remove any cooked-on food, but do not leave the cooking pot immersed in the sink; just fill with warm soapy water and let soak until the cooked-on food comes away freely. (Some

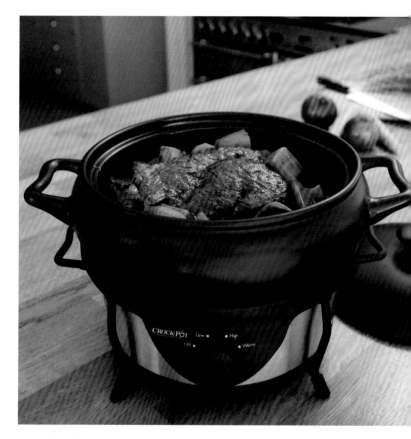

models feature dishwasher-safe pots, so check your manual.) Pack your slow cooker away only when it is completely cool, clean and thoroughly dry.

TIP

Your slow cooker is an invaluable way to use up leftovers. Odds and ends of vegetables can make a great base for a soup, or add a selection of pulses/legumes and leftover cooked meats for an economical meal.

getting started

It is exciting using a piece of kitchen equipment for the first time. Take your time and don't rush into cooking anything until you have read the instruction manual thoroughly. It may take a little time to get used to using a slow cooker, as it can be quite different from other cooking methods. After unpacking your new slow cooker, make sure you wash the inner ceramic pot and the lid with warm soapy water. Dry thoroughly. Find a position in your kitchen where the slow cooker will be safe. Make sure the cable can be tucked away and the unit is out of the way of children as the housing may become hot.

When you are deciding what to cook in your slow cooker, choose a recipe that will fit within the capacity of your cooker. Before you start your recipe, make sure that any dishes, bowls or pans you are using fit inside the cooker first. Imagine making a meatloaf and finding the loaf pan does not fit in your slow cooker. If you intend to finish a dish under the grill/broiler, check the instruction manual first to see if you can put the cooking pot under a direct heat source.

How full should the pot be?

Liquids are the most important component when cooking in a slow cooker. There should always be liquid to start the cooking off with. Stews and casseroles generate liquid as they cook because of the water content of the food and the steaming that occurs during cooking time. This means that you could add only 100 ml/scant ½ cup of water, stock or wine and find you have as much as 400 ml/ scant 2 cups at the end of the cooking time.

A joint of meat or chicken should not take up any more than three-quarters of the cooking pot, while a pan, baking dish or bowl should have about 2.5 cm/1 inch of space around it with the water

coming roughly halfway up the side of the basin. When cooking soups, make sure that the liquid has a clearance of no less than 3 cm/1¼ inches from the top of the pot.

Do I need to preheat the slow cooker?

Refer to your manufacturer's instruction manual, as some recommend a preheating time and others recommend switching the slow cooker to the desired setting only when it is filled with food.

Cooking times and heat settings

Timings and settings vary for the type of dish or cut of meat you are using, or how long you need your dish to cook for to fit in with your day: your slow cooker really can be used to suit your lifestyle and pace.

The LOW setting essentially suits smaller cuts of meat and dishes with ingredients that need gentle cooking. The low setting will eventually reach the same temperature as HIGH, but just take a much longer time to do so.

LOW is good for:
- Diced meats, chicken joints, chops and cutlets
- Soups
- Bain marie method of cooking
- Fish or vegetable casseroles and curries

The HIGH setting can be used in a variety of ways, e.g. cooking large pieces of meat or if you want your dish to be cooked in a shorter time. As a rule, it will take half the time to cook a stew or casserole on HIGH than on the LOW setting. When thickening stews or casseroles, increase the temperature from LOW to HIGH, add your cornflour/cornstarch, and cook for a further 20 minutes.

HIGH is good for:
- Whole joints of meat or whole birds
- Steamed dishes or cakes and anything with a rising agent, such as dumplings
- Pâtés and terrines
- Soups

Some machines have an AUTO setting, which means the cooker starts off on HIGH then automatically turns itself down to LOW after a set time – this is great for giving your cooking an initial boost.

A WARM setting will keep your food hot if your mealtime is delayed, although it is not an essential setting. Keeping the cooker on LOW would not overcook your food, even if left for an extra few hours. The exception to this rule is if a dish contains pasta or rice.

Adjusting timings

If you want to speed up or slow down casseroles based on diced meat or vegetables, so that the cooking fits around your schedule, adjust the heat settings and timings as below.

LOW	MEDIUM	HIGH
6–8 hours	4–6 hours	3–4 hours
8–10 hours	6–8 hours	5–6 hours
10–12 hours	8–10 hours	7–8 hours

TIP

Don't be tempted to lift the lid of the slow cooker, as this breaks the seal created by the steam between the lid and the cooking pot. Each time the lid is lifted, you should add an extra 20 minutes to the total cooking time.

preparing food for the slow cooker

Good preparation of ingredients is key to using a slow cooker. Be well prepared and have everything ready the night before, if necessary.

Meat

Cheap cuts of meat are perfect for use in a slow cooker. For casseroles and stews, make sure the chunks of meat are cut to the same size. Forgotten cuts such as pig's cheeks or pork shanks are great for this method of cooking. Browning the meat will add flavour and colour to the finished dish, but it is not imperative. For a healthier dish, or if you are short on time, just add the meat raw. Whole birds or joints need to be cooked only on HIGH, but any other cut can be used on a setting to suit when you require it. Remove skin and fat from meats otherwise you may have a build up of liquid fat in your finished dishes.

Vegetables

Cut all vegetables the same size when preparing them for the slow cooker. Onions need softening in a little oil first, otherwise they tend to retain a bit of a bite, but other vegetables can go straight into the pot. Root vegetables can take longer to cook than the meat, so make sure these are cut smaller than the chunks of meat for even and consistent cooking.

Fish

Fish responds really well in a slow cooker when cooked on LOW. The gentle cooking of this setting means the fish stays intact. Poach large fillets of fish or cook chunks of fish in a sauce. As shellfish only require a little cooking, add these for a short time at the end of cooking. Turn the slow cooker onto HIGH and cook for the last 15–20 minutes of the cooking time for your dish.

Pasta

Pasta will become unpleasantly stodgy, absorbing too much liquid if added at the beginning of the cooking time. Either cook in boiling water and stir through the finished dish to warm through or add for the last 30–40 minutes of cooking time only.

Rice

Rice can quickly become overcooked in a slow cooker as the grains split apart, but with a little experience it can be very easy to prepare well. Easy-cook rice is the best choice as it has been pre-washed and partially cooked by the manufacturer, giving you a less starchy finish. Basmati and long-grain can work well, too. Add rice to dishes 25–30 minutes from end of cooking time. The only exception here is rice puddings.

TIP

Foods at the bottom of the cooking pot will cook faster so think about how you assemble your dish when adding it to the pot.

Pulses/Legumes

Dried pulses/legumes contain a toxin if not cooked properly, so it is important to follow the correct method when using these in your slow cooker. Soak overnight, then boil for at least 10 minutes before adding to the slow cooker. Exceptions to this rule are lentils and pearl barley, which can be added directly.

Cream and milk

Dishes such as rice pudding or baked/caramel custard will cook very well in your slow cooker, but whole milk or cream will be less likely to split or curdle than skimmed dairy products due to the fat content. Always use whole milk and whipping or double/heavy cream. If you are making a creamy soup, always stir the cream through 15 minutes before the end of cooking time, not before.

TIP

Think about substituting canned pulses/legumes for dried. Slow cooking is all about economy and convenience, so the quicker the preparation of your dish, the more time you have to spend doing other things.

getting the most from your slow cooker

Your slow cooker is a very versatile piece of kitchen equipment that you will want to keep on using again and again. Don't just think about your slow cooker for making stews and casseroles. A slow cooker can also work like a conventional bain marie, so it can be used for making baked custards and sweet or savoury dishes. The generous capacity of most models also makes it ideal for making large batches of chutneys and preserves. What about using it to make a rich, flavoursome chicken stock for use in soups?

Adapting your own recipes for a slow cooker

Adapting your own favourite recipes for a slow cooker is a simple process of comparison. Look for a similar recipe within this book which will give you an idea of how to prepare the ingredients and the approximate amounts you may need. Finding a similar recipe will also help you to determine the cooking time required. Reduce any liquids within your own recipe by at least half, making sure the ingredients are covered by about two thirds. Using fresh ingredients that contain lots of water (such as fresh tomatoes) will create liquid so you will need to add even less stock or water to the recipe to accommodate this.

Changing recipes to suit different models of slow cooker

If you need to adapt a recipe, it may be that you need to halve it for a small machine, or add half as much again to feed a larger crowd from a big slow cooker. The larger quantity may take a while longer to come up to heat. Therefore, if you are intending on cooking the recipe on LOW, start it off on HIGH for 30–60 minutes or set the cooker to AUTO to allow the food to reach the correct temperature more quickly. However, the actual

TIP

Make sure that any stock or water you add to your recipe is hot to get the cooking temperature up to speed as soon as possible.

cooking timings remain the same. If you are unsure of your slow cooker's capacity, measure with a jug/cups and water then you can roughly work out from the ingredient list the final quantity of your recipe.

Cooking for the freezer

Using a slow cooker is the perfect way to create 'convenience' food of your very own. Whether you live on your own or lead a busy family lifestyle, use your slow cooker to batch-cook soups, casseroles, or stews. When cooling the food, it is important to do this as quickly as possible, so remove it from the slow cooker and transfer to freezerproof containers or freezer bags, uncovered or unsealed, then let cool. Cover, then freeze straight away. Defrost the portions in a fridge overnight or for about 4 hours at room temperature. Always reheat thoroughly until very hot before serving. You can do this in a pan on the hob/stovetop, or in a microwave. With a little forward planning, you need never be without a good meal from your slow cooker.

TIP

If adding wine to a recipe, especially red, reduce it in a saucepan set over the hob/stovetop by at least a quarter to cook out the alcohol before adding to the slow cooker. The temperature within the slow cooker is not hot enough to do this and can result in a bitter-tasting dish.

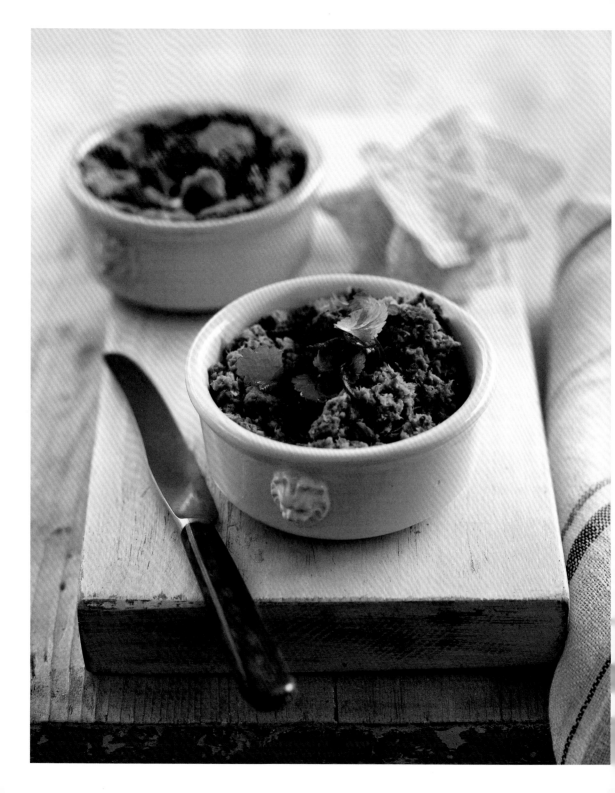

SOUPS, APPETIZERS & LIGHT BITES

Italian pasta & bean soup

2 tablespoons olive oil

1 large onion, finely chopped

2 garlic cloves, finely chopped

1 large potato, peeled and diced

4 ripe tomatoes, coarsely chopped

1 tablespoon tomato purée/paste

1.25 litres/5 cups chicken or vegetable stock

a sprig of fresh thyme, sage or rosemary

2 x 400-g/14-oz. cans cannellini beans, drained and rinsed

150 g/5 oz. small dried pasta shapes, such as orecchiette

a pinch of dried red chilli/hot pepper flakes

sea salt and freshly ground black pepper

freshly grated Parmesan cheese, to serve

SERVES 4

This hearty soup of pasta and beans is a classic from the region of Puglia in Italy. The pasta shapes traditionally used are orecchiette, meaning 'little ears', but you can use any shape you have to hand.

Heat the oil in a large saucepan, add the onion, garlic and potato, and cook for 3–4 minutes until golden. Add the tomatoes, tomato purée/paste, stock, herbs and beans. Season to taste then transfer to a slow cooker, cover and cook on HIGH for 3½ hours.

Remove the lid, add the pasta and chilli/pepper flakes and stir. Cook for a further 20–30 minutes depending upon what pasta shapes you use, or until the pasta is al dente. Ladle into bowls and serve sprinkled with a little Parmesan.

chicken soup

*A bowlful of this traditional comforting soup makes everyone feel better,
especially when served with plenty of warmed bread.*

1 tablespoon olive oil

1 onion, chopped

1 garlic clove, crushed

2 chicken breasts, diced

2 leeks, well cleaned and chopped

200 g/7 oz. potatoes, unpeeled
and chopped

1 litre/4 cups hot chicken stock

3 sprigs of fresh thyme

2 dried bay leaves

200-g can/1 cup sweetcorn/
corn kernels, drained

sea salt and freshly ground
black pepper

SERVES 4

Heat the olive oil in a saucepan, add the onion, garlic, chicken and
leeks, and sauté gently for 8 minutes without browning. Add the
potatoes, hot stock, thyme and bay leaves, then season lightly.

Transfer the ingredients to the slow cooker, cover with the lid and
cook on HIGH for 4 hours. About 1 hour before serving, stir in the
(sweet) corn. Remove the thyme and bay leaves and check the
seasoning before serving.

golden butternut squash soup

Squash is a wonderfully versatile and delicious vegetable, and it's used to great effect in this flavourful soup.

1-kg/2¼-lb. butternut squash, peeled

2 tablespoons olive oil

2 onions, chopped

1 garlic clove, crushed

1.25 litres/5 cups chicken or vegetable stock

sea salt and freshly ground black pepper

single/light cream, to serve (optional)

SERVES 4

Cut the squash in half lengthwise and use a spoon to scoop out the seeds. Chop the squash into 2.5-cm/1-inch pieces.

Heat the oil in a large saucepan, add the onions and garlic and sauté over low heat for 10 minutes. Add the chopped squash pieces and the stock and bring to the boil.

Transfer to the slow cooker, cover with the lid, and cook on HIGH for 1 hour.

Using a hand-held blender or liquidizer, blitz the soup until smooth and creamy. Season to taste and serve with a swirl of cream, if liked.

garlic & chilli/chile rice soup with wilted greens

This is a substantial soup – really more of a light stew. Boiled rice soups are popular in many Asian countries, especially China. Instead of the spring/collard greens, you can use the fresh, young outer leaves of any brassicas, such as cabbage. They work very nicely with the simple Asian flavours here.

2 tablespoons vegetable oil

4 teaspoons sesame oil

4 garlic cloves, chopped

8 spring onions/scallions, finely chopped

4 teaspoons finely grated fresh ginger

2 small red fresh chillies/chiles, seeded and thinly sliced

200 g/½ cup long-grain white rice

1.5 litres/6 cups vegetable stock

2 tablespoons soy sauce or Thai fish sauce

a bunch of spring/collard greens, roughly shredded

a small handful of chopped fresh coriander/cilantro

ground white pepper

SERVES 4

Put the oils in a saucepan and set over high heat. Add the garlic and spring onions/scallions and cook until the garlic is turning golden (burnt garlic is very bitter and not nice at all). This will give the soup a lovely nutty garlic flavour. Add the ginger, chillies/chiles and rice to the pan and stir-fry in the garlic-infused oil for 1 minute. Add the stock and soy sauce and bring to the boil.

Transfer to the slow cooker, cover with the lid, and cook on HIGH for 1½ hours. Add the chopped greens and cook for a further 30 minutes until they turn emerald green and are tender. Ladle the soup into warmed serving bowls, sprinkle the coriander/cilantro over the top and season to taste with white pepper.

Scotch broth

From the land that brings us haggis, kippers, neeps and tatties comes its famous namesake broth. Barley is traditionally used but this recipe features wholesome brown rice – use whichever you prefer.

2 tablespoons light olive oil

2 carrots, chopped

1 leek, well cleaned and chopped

2 celery stalks, chopped, including leaves

500 g/1 lb. stewing lamb, well trimmed of fat and cut into small cubes

1 litre/4 cups hot chicken stock

1 tablespoon light soy sauce

95 g/½ cup brown rice

sea salt and freshly ground black pepper

soft white/dinner rolls, buttered, to serve

SERVES 4

Heat the oil in a large saucepan. Add the carrots, leek, celery and celery leaves and cook over high heat for 5 minutes, stirring often. Add the lamb and cook for a further 5 minutes until the meat is browned.

Transfer the vegetables and lamb to the slow cooker. Add the hot chicken stock and soy sauce. Cover with the lid and cook on HIGH for 2 hours until the vegetables are cooked. Add the brown rice, replace the lid and cook for 1 hour further.

Season to taste and serve with soft buttered rolls.

classic minestrone

1 tablespoon olive oil

1 red onion, chopped

2 garlic cloves, crushed

2 leeks, well cleaned and sliced

2 carrots, chopped

2 celery stalks, chopped

4 thick slices of bacon, chopped

400-g/14-oz. can haricot/navy or cannellini beans, drained and rinsed

1.25 litres/5 cups chicken or vegetable stock

1½ tablespoons tomato purée/paste

1 dried bay leaf

a small bunch of fresh thyme

75 g/½ cup tiny pasta shapes

fresh pesto or freshly grated Parmesan, to serve (optional)

SERVES 4

This classic Italian soup is always popular and is the perfect recipe for cooking in a slow cooker. Serve with a swirl of fresh pesto or freshly grated Parmesan.

Heat the oil in a saucepan, add the onion, garlic, leeks, carrots, celery and bacon, and sauté for 10 minutes over medium heat without browning.

Add the beans, stock, tomato purée/paste and herbs, bring to the boil and transfer to the slow cooker. Cover with the lid and cook on HIGH for 2 hours. Add the pasta shapes, replace the lid and cook for a further 30 minutes.

Season and serve with a spoonful of pesto and some Parmesan, if using.

slow cooker stock

2 carcasses uncooked chicken, 1 kg/
2¼ lbs. wings, or 1 turkey drumstick,
sliced

any giblets or trimmings, such as
wingtips from the chickens

4 carrots, sliced

1 leek, well cleaned and sliced

1 onion, sliced or chopped

1 celery stalk, sliced

1 teaspoon black peppercorns

1 fresh bay leaf

a sprig of fresh thyme

2–3 fresh parsley stalks

2 tablespoons white wine or
1 tablespoon white wine vinegar

MAKES ABOUT
2 LITRES/QUARTS

*A slow cooker is a convenient way to make an all-
purpose fresh chicken stock, which can be frozen and
stored for use in a wide variety of recipes, such as
soups and casseroles.*

Put all the ingredients in the slow cooker, cover with cold water
and cook on LOW for at least 12 hours or overnight.

Strain, leave to cool and freeze in smaller portions for convenience.

blue cheese fondue

This flavourful blue cheese fondue is perfect served as an appetizer with asparagus tips or grissini for dipping, or even as a dessert with pears and fresh walnuts.

125 ml/½ cup sweet white wine such as German Riesling or Gewürztraminer

400 g/14 oz. creamy blue cheese, such as Gorgonzola or Roquefort, coarsely chopped

1 teaspoon cornflour/cornstarch mixed with 1 tablespoon of the wine

to serve

24 asparagus spears, lightly cooked and grissini (breadsticks) or 4–6 ripe pears, quartered, and fresh walnuts

SERVES 6

To prepare the fondue, pour the wine into the slow cooker and heat on HIGH until warm – this may take 30 minutes.

Switch to LOW and gradually stir in the blue cheese followed by the cornflour/cornstarch mixture. Stir constantly for about 45 minutes until the cheese has melted and the mixture is smooth.

Serve either with grissini and asparagus for dipping or with ripe pears and fresh walnuts for dessert.

smoked & fresh salmon terrine

250 g/9 oz. skinless salmon fillet, cut into chunks

1 teaspoon finely grated orange zest

2 teaspoons fresh orange juice

4 tablespoons chopped fresh dill

350 g/12 oz. smoked salmon

2 egg whites, chilled and lightly whisked

150 ml/⅔ cup whipping/heavy cream, chilled

freshly ground white pepper

baby salad leaves/greens, to serve

hazelnut dressing

3 tablespoons olive oil

1 tablespoon hazelnut oil

½ tablespoon freshly squeezed lemon juice

2 tablespoons chopped hazelnuts

2 tablespoons chopped fresh parsley

sea salt and freshly ground black pepper

a loaf pan or terrine mould, about 850-ml/3-cup capacity, lightly oiled and base-lined with baking parchment

SERVES 6

A mousseline is a mousse of fish, shellfish or poultry lightened with cream and egg whites. When made with salmon, it is the most beautiful elegant golden-pink. It is amazingly easy to prepare in a slow cooker too, with a spectacular effect that makes a very luxurious appetizer or posh picnic dish.

Put the chunks of fresh salmon into a food processor with the orange zest, orange juice, dill and plenty of white pepper. Blend until smooth. Remove the bowl from the food processor, cover and chill.

Meanwhile, roughly chop half the smoked salmon. Put the bowl back on the processor. With the machine running, add the egg whites through the tube, then the cream. Blend until thick and smooth – do not overwork or it will curdle. Scrape into a bowl and stir in the chopped smoked salmon.

Carefully fill the prepared loaf pan with the mixture, packing it down well. Level the surface and cover the top with buttered baking parchment. Stand in the slow cooker and pour in enough hot water to come halfway up the sides. Cover with the lid and cook on HIGH for 2 hours until firm.

Remove from the slow cooker, let cool completely, then chill in the refrigerator. Loosen the edges with a thin knife and turn out onto a board. Trim and tidy up the edges and pat dry. Wrap the terrine with the remaining smoked salmon, pressing down well, then transfer to a flat serving platter.

Put the salad in a small bowl, whisk the dressing ingredients together, then pour over the leaves/greens and toss gently. Slice the terrine with a very sharp knife and serve with the salad.

pork, fennel & spinach terrine

This is a chunky terrine of pork, flavoured with fennel seeds and layered with spinach. Its small size makes it perfect for a small party of guests or to serve for a simple snack or lunch.

2 fresh bay leaves

150 g/5 oz. dry-cured streaky/fatty bacon

100 g/2 cups fresh spinach, chopped

2 tablespoons olive oil

1 small onion, chopped

1 teaspoon fennel seeds, crushed

2 garlic cloves, finely chopped

300 g/10 oz. pork belly, coarsely minced/ground

200 g/7 oz. lean pork fillet/tenderloin, diced

½ teaspoon ground nutmeg

½ teaspoon ground allspice

1 teaspoon sea salt

½ teaspoon black pepper

crusty bread, to serve

a loaf pan or terrine mould, about 850-ml/3-cup capacity, lightly oiled

SERVES 6

Arrange the bay leaves over the bottom of the loaf pan, then lay enough bacon across the width to cover the base, reserving any slices left to cover the top of the terrine later. Put the spinach in a colander and pour over boiling water to blanch. Refresh with cold water, squeeze out any excess water and set aside.

Heat the olive oil in a frying pan/skillet over low heat and sauté the onion, fennel seeds and garlic for 3–5 minutes, or until soft but not yet brown. Transfer to a large bowl with half of the spinach, the minced/ground pork and fillet/tenderloin, nutmeg and allspice. Add the salt and pepper and mix well.

Put half of the pork mixture in the prepared loaf pan and press down firmly. Top with the remaining spinach, then the remaining pork mixture. Press down firmly, then fold over any overhanging bacon and use the reserved slices to cover the top of the terrine. Tightly cover with oiled foil and sit in the slow cooker. Fill the slow cooker with enough water to come halfway up the sides of the terrine. Cover the slow cooker with the lid and cook on HIGH for 4 hours.

Transfer to a dish to catch any juices and put a weight on top. Let cool, then chill overnight or for 1–2 days. Serve with crusty bread.

beef & ale pâté

This pâté is great party fare. It was inspired by 'tinga', a dish of Mexican shredded beef, and relies on slow cooking and a few key flavours. Even though it calls for a cheap cut of beef, it pays to use the best quality you can find.

2 tablespoons olive oil

5 large, mild fresh red chillies/chiles

3 whole garlic cloves, peeled

600 g/1¼ lbs. chuck/blade steak, trimmed of fat and cut into 2.5-cm/ 1-inch chunks

2 x 330-ml/12-oz. bottles of ale

400-g/14-oz. can pinto beans, drained

sea salt

a handful of chopped fresh coriander/ cilantro, to garnish

tortilla chips, to serve

MAKES ABOUT 750 ML/3 CUPS

Heat the olive oil in a large, heavy-based saucepan set over medium/low heat. Cut the green stalk ends from 3 of the red chillies/chiles. Put these chillies/chiles and the garlic in the saucepan and gently cook for 3 minutes. Increase the heat to medium/high, add the steak, and cook, stirring occasionally, for 5 minutes until the meat is browned.

Add the ale to the saucepan and bring to the boil. Transfer the ingredients to the slow cooker and cover with the lid. Cook for 7 hours on HIGH. About 2 hours before the end of cooking time, add the canned beans and stir well. The meat should be falling apart at the end of the cooking time.

Put the meat with its accompanying ingredients and a little of the cooking liquid in a food processor and process briefly until you have a coarse pâté. Season to taste with salt. Spoon into a serving dish. Cut the remaining red chillies/chiles into thin strips and scatter over the pâté along with the coriander/cilantro. Serve warm or at room temperature with tortilla chips for dipping.

spinach & ricotta timbales

These are like little savoury cheesecakes, served warm with a drizzle of olive oil or a small spoonful of rich tomato sauce. Straining the ricotta makes the mixture lighter, so is worth the additional effort. Beat the eggs into the cheese very well for even more lightness, and be careful with the seasoning – the capers and olives are both quite salty already.

10 sun-dried (or sun-blushed) tomatoes in oil, drained

250 g/9 oz. fresh spinach

500 g/1 lb. 2.oz. ricotta, well drained

3 large eggs, beaten

12 small Greek-style black olives, pitted and coarsely chopped

2 tablespoons chopped fresh basil or oregano

2 tablespoons salted capers, rinsed and chopped, plus extra whole capers to serve

freshly grated nutmeg

sea salt and freshly ground black pepper

olive oil or fresh tomato sauce, to serve

6 dariole moulds or 125-ml/½-cup capacity ramekins, well buttered

SERVES 6

Put a sun-dried tomato in the bottom of each mould or ramekin. Thinly slice the remaining sun-dried tomatoes.

To prepare the spinach, remove the tough stems from the leaves, then wash the leaves really well and put in a saucepan while still wet. Cook until the leaves wilt, then plunge into cold water. Drain very well and squeeze to extract any excess moisture. Loosen the leaves slightly.

Push the ricotta through a fine-mesh sieve/strainer to make it fluffy, then beat in the eggs. Lightly stir in the drained, wilted spinach, sliced sun-dried tomatoes, olives, basil or oregano, and capers. Taste and season lightly with salt, pepper, and nutmeg.

Spoon the ricotta mixture into the moulds and level, then put them in the slow cooker. Carefully fill the slow cooker with boiling water to come halfway up the moulds. Cover and cook on HIGH for 50 minutes until almost set and a little puffed. Remove from the slow cooker and let cool slightly. Turn out onto small plates, then serve at room temperature with extra capers and a sprinkle of olive oil or a spoonful of fresh tomato sauce.

eggs cocotte

These baked eggs go down a treat at breakfast, brunch or as a light dinner. If you can't fit four ramekins in your slow cooker you could try placing one on top of the others as it should still cook well.

60 g/2 oz. fresh spinach, chopped

4 large eggs

4 tablespoons milk

75 g/¾ cup grated Parmesan cheese

sea salt and freshly ground black pepper

hot buttered toast, to serve

4 ovenproof ramekins, buttered

SERVES 4

Divide the spinach between the prepared ramekins. Crack an egg on top, add a spoonful of milk to each, then season and top with the grated Parmesan. Place in the slow cooker and pour in enough boiling water to come halfway up the dishes. Cover with the lid and cook for 35–40 minutes on HIGH, until the eggs have set.

Serve with hot buttered toast.

MEAT DISHES

Yankee pot roast

The pot roast is one of the great American classics and when it appears with braised vegetables, it becomes Yankee pot roast. Serve with a big mound of creamy mashed potatoes.

3 tablespoons oil or bacon fat

1 tablespoon ground allspice

1 teaspoon sea salt

2 tablespoons plain/all-purpose flour

1 tablespoon dry mustard

1 kg/2¼ lbs. rolled silverside/boneless beef chuck

150 ml/⅔ cup red wine

100 ml/scant ½ cup beef stock

4 parsnips, cut into 5-cm/2-inch chunks

2 sweet potatoes, cut into 5-cm/2-inch chunks

2 carrots, cut into 5-cm/2-inch chunks

12 small red onions, cut into 4 wedges through the root

2 tablespoons cornflour/cornstarch

sea salt and freshly ground black pepper

creamy mashed potatoes, to serve

SERVES 4

Put 1 tablespoon of the oil, the allspice, salt, flour and mustard in a small bowl and mix to form a paste, adding more oil as necessary. Rub the beef with the mixture, cover and marinate in the fridge for 3 hours or overnight.

Remove the meat and shake off any excess spices. Heat the remaining oil or bacon fat in a large frying pan/skillet, add the meat and brown on all sides. Transfer to the slow cooker.

Add the wine to the frying pan/skillet, bring to the boil and cook until reduced by two-thirds. Pour over the meat along with the stock, cover with the lid and cook on HIGH for 7 hours.

Add the vegetables and cook for 1 further hour. Mix the cornflour/cornstarch with 3 tablespoons water and blend it into the gravy. Cook for a further 15 minutes, then serve with some creamy mashed potatoes.

chili con carne

2 tablespoons olive oil

2 onions, chopped

3 garlic cloves, crushed

700 g/1½ lbs. lean minced/ground beef

2 tablespoons tomato purée/paste

600 ml/2⅓ cups passata (Italian strained tomatoes)

1 tablespoon cayenne pepper

1 tablespoon Spanish smoked sweet paprika (pimentón dulce)

2 x 400-g/14-oz. cans red kidney beans, drained and rinsed

sea salt and freshly ground black pepper

to serve

3 tablespoons chopped fresh coriander/cilantro leaves

boiled white rice

guacamole (optional)

sour cream (optional)

SERVES 4–6

Long, slow cooking is the secret of good chili. Simple dishes are often the best, and they don't come much simpler than this. You can add more or less cayenne pepper, depending on how hot you like your food.

Heat the oil in a large saucepan, add the onions and garlic and sauté gently for 5 minutes. Add the beef, breaking it up with a wooden spoon, and cook for a further 5 minutes or until browned. Add the beef mixture to the slow cooker and stir in the tomato purée/paste, passata, cayenne pepper and paprika and season well.

Cover with the lid and cook on HIGH for 5 hours, adding the kidney beans 1 hour before the end of cooking time just to warm them through.

Just before serving, stir in the chopped coriander/cilantro and serve with rice and guacamole and sour cream, if liked.

meatloaf with tomato sauce

Here, a classic meatloaf is served with a delicious tomato sauce. All it needs is a side of green beans to make a satisfying family meal.

12 slices of Parma ham or prosciutto

200 g/7 oz. chicken livers, chopped

400 g/14 oz. lean pork, chopped

300 g/10 oz. minced/ground turkey or chicken

1 red onion, chopped

2 eggs, beaten

3 fresh bay leaves, torn

a bunch of fresh flat-leaf parsley, chopped

sea salt and freshly ground black pepper

green beans and butter/lima beans, to serve (optional)

tomato sauce

3 tablespoons olive oil

1 onion, chopped

2 garlic cloves, crushed

2 x 400-g/14-oz. cans chopped tomatoes

900-g/2-lb. loaf pan

SERVES 6

Line the loaf pan with the Parma ham, leaving some aside to cover the top of the finished meatloaf.

Put the chicken livers in a bowl with the pork and turkey, add the onion, eggs, bay leaves and parsley, season and mix well. This is best done with your hands.

Fill the prepared pan with the meat, level the top and cover with the remaining ham. Cover with foil and place in the slow cooker. Carefully pour in enough boiling water to come halfway up the sides of the pan and cook on HIGH for 4 hours. Remove and let stand for 10 minutes. Drain off any juice into a jug/pitcher, then turn out the meatloaf onto a deep plate.

To make the tomato sauce, heat the oil and sauté the onion gently for 5 minutes in a saucepan. Add the garlic and cook for a further 5 minutes. Add the tomatoes and reserved meat juices, season and simmer gently for 30 minutes, stirring frequently. Serve the sauce alongside slices of the meatloaf, with green beans and butter/lima beans, if you like.

Notes: If you prefer your meatloaf a bit browner, place it in an oven preheated to 200°C (400°F) Gas 6 for 10 minutes to brown before serving. If your slow cooker cannot take a 900-g/2-lb. pan, divide the mixture into two portions and cook one portion in a 450-g/1-lb. loaf pan, adjusting the cooking time to 3 hours. Freeze the second portion and cook another time.

Provençal daube of beef

Daubes are dishes in which the meat is simmered in wine for a long time and is so soft that it can be cut with a spoon. The wine used here is a white one, which is rather unexpected with beef. It gives a more acid pungency to the dish and goes well with the traditional olives.

4 tablespoons olive oil

500 g/1 lb. 2 oz. onions, sliced

2 garlic cloves, sliced

2 tomatoes, chopped

1 carrot, sliced crossways

2 sprigs of fresh thyme

2 fresh bay leaves

1 kg/2¼ lbs. rolled rib of beef/boneless beef rib-eye, in one piece

100 ml/scant ½ cup white wine

6 green olives, pitted

6 black olives, pitted

sea salt and freshly ground black pepper

to serve

creamy mashed potatoes

steamed baby carrots

SERVES 4

Heat 2 tablespoons of the oil in a large frying pan/skillet. Add the onions and sauté until softened but not browned. Add the garlic, tomatoes, carrot, thyme and bay leaves and sauté until lightly browned. Transfer to the slow cooker. Add the remaining oil and beef to the frying pan/skillet, brown it on all sides then transfer to the slow cooker.

Pour the wine into the frying pan/skillet, scraping any brown bits into the liquid. Season with salt and pepper and pour this mixture over the beef. Cover with the lid and cook on LOW for 8–10 hours. Add the olives to the casserole for the last 30 minutes of cooking time just to heat through.

Serve with lots of creamy mashed potatoes and a few steamed baby carrots – the beef should be so tender that it falls to pieces when touched.

Irish carbonnade

750 g/1½ lbs. skirt/flank steak, cut into 3-cm/1½-inch cubes

3 tablespoons soft brown sugar

1 onion, chopped

4 tablespoons plain/all-purpose flour

12 shallots, peeled

500 ml/2 cups beef stock

375 ml/1½ cups dark Irish stout, such as Guinness

2 tablespoons red wine vinegar

3 cloves

1 fresh or 2 dried bay leaves

sea salt and freshly ground black pepper

a handful of chopped fresh flat-leaf parsley, to garnish

Irish Cheddar croûtes

12 slices of baguette

olive oil, for drizzling

150 g/5 oz. strong/sharp Cheddar cheese (preferably Irish), grated

SERVES 4

Carbonnades are native to Belgium and northern France, where they are always flavoured with beer, but a good Irish stout actually gives an even tastier result. Lots of sweet shallots or pickling onions add a little sweetness and balance the flavours nicely.

Put all the carbonnade ingredients in the slow cooker and mix well. Cover with the lid and cook on HIGH for 6–7 hours until the meat is tender.

To make the Irish Cheddar croûtes, preheat the oven to 200°C (400°F) Gas 6. Arrange the baguette slices on a baking sheet and drizzle both sides with olive oil. Toast in the preheated oven for about 5 minutes until golden brown. Remove from the oven, pile each croûte with grated cheese, and return to the oven to cook until the cheese has melted.

Serve the carbonnade sprinkled with parsley and with the hot croûtes alongside.

Greek braised lamb with okra

This is a very simple dish but surprisingly effective considering how few ingredients there are, so make sure you adjust the seasoning carefully as it makes such a difference. Ideally, each steak should be about 2.5 cm/ 1 inch thick and weigh about 250 g/9 oz. Trim the stem end only of the okra, taking off the tiniest layer of the already-cut surface, to discourage the sticky liquid from oozing out.

3 tablespoons olive oil

4 lamb steaks, about 1 kg/2¼ lbs., cut from the leg and deboned

1 small onion, sliced

2 garlic cloves, crushed

4 tomatoes, skinned, seeded and chopped

175 g/6 oz. okra, trimmed

sea salt and freshly ground black pepper

boiled new potatoes, to serve

a handful of chopped fresh flat-leaf parsley, to garnish

SERVES 4

Heat the oil in a large saucepan. Season the meat with salt and pepper, add to the saucepan and brown the pieces all over. Use a slotted spoon to transfer the browned meat to the slow cooker.

Add the onion and garlic to the saucepan and cook until softened and lightly browned. Add the tomatoes and simmer until they are soft and pulpy. Add the tomato mixture to the lamb steaks in the slow cooker, turning the lamb steaks over to ensure the meat is well coated.

Cover with the lid and cook on HIGH for 3 hours. After 2 hours, add the prepared okra, tucking the fingers under the lamb steaks so that they are coated with sauce. Cook for 1 further hour, check the seasoning and adjust if necessary. Serve with new potatoes sprinkled with the chopped parsley.

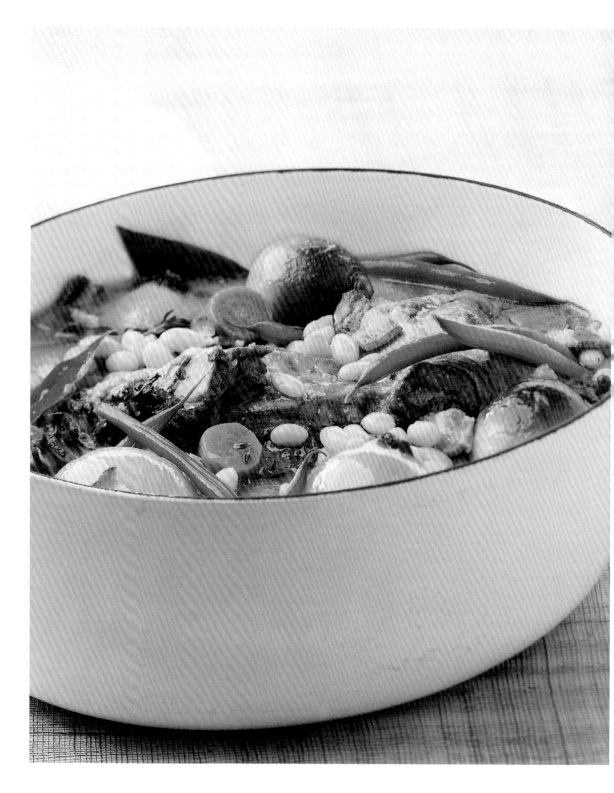

Tuscan pork & bean casserole

A 'hand' of pork is part of the shoulder of the animal. It is often considered the best part for roasting or braising, as it has just the right amount of fat, whereas the leg is so lean as to make it difficult to keep moist. Anyway, a certain amount of fat is needed in this dish to moisten the beans – or perhaps it's the other way round and the beans are needed to mop up the juices. Either way, it makes for a scrumptious dinner.

4 tablespoons olive oil

350 g/12 oz. carrots, cut into 2.5-cm/
1-inch chunks

4 onions, peeled but left whole

4 small turnips, peeled but left whole

1 sprig of fresh thyme

1 dried or fresh bay leaf

6 peppercorns

6 garlic cloves, or to taste, crushed

2-kg/4½-lb. hand of pork (picnic
shoulder), rind removed

250 g/9 oz. smoked streaky bacon in
one piece, cut into chunks

400-g/14-oz. can cannellini beans,
drained and rinsed

450 g/1 lb. new potatoes, peeled

250 g/9 oz. green beans

sea salt and freshly ground
black pepper

SERVES 4

Heat the oil in a large saucepan, then add the carrots, onions, turnips, thyme, bay leaf, peppercorns and garlic. Sauté gently without browning for 10–15 minutes. Transfer to the slow cooker.

Add the pork and its rind and the bacon chunks to the slow cooker. Cover with boiling water, add salt and pepper, cover with the lid, and cook on HIGH for 3 hours. Add the cannellini beans and cook for 1 further hour. Add the potatoes for the last 30 minutes and the fresh green beans for the last 5 minutes of cooking time. (If space in your slow cooker is limited, simply cook these separately on the hob/stovetop and serve them on the side.)

To serve, remove and discard the pork rind, lift the meat onto a dish and carve into thick slices. Add the vegetables and green beans to the dish (if cooked separately) and serve with a separate small jug/pitcher of the cooking juices.

Lancashire hotpot

500 g/1 lb. 2 oz. braising steak, trimmed of fat

250 g/9 oz. shoulder of lamb, trimmed of fat

2 lamb's kidneys, cleaned and trimmed (optional)

2 tablespoons plain/all-purpose flour

1 onion, thinly sliced

1 carrot, cut into chunks

1 fresh or dried bay leaf

350 g/12 oz. potatoes, cut into chunks

300 ml/1¼ cups boiling beef stock

½ teaspoon sea salt

1 teaspoon sugar

¼ teaspoon freshly ground black pepper

1 teaspoon anchovy essence or sauce

green beans, to serve

SERVES 4

A traditional British hotpot was an earthenware vessel with a tight-fitting lid, tall enough to take whole cuts of lamb standing upright, so it was very tall! Nowadays a slow cooker will do the job very well, as the name refers to the contents rather than the pot. The version from Lancashire in the North of England usually contains beef as well as lamb.

Cut the steak, lamb and kidneys, if using, into 2.5-cm/1-inch pieces and sprinkle with the flour. Arrange them in the slow cooker.

Add the onion, carrot and bay leaf, then put the potatoes on top in a layer. Mix together the boiling stock with the salt, sugar, pepper and anchovy essence and pour the liquid over everything in the slow cooker. Cover with the lid and cook on HIGH for 4–5 hours.

Serve hot with green beans.

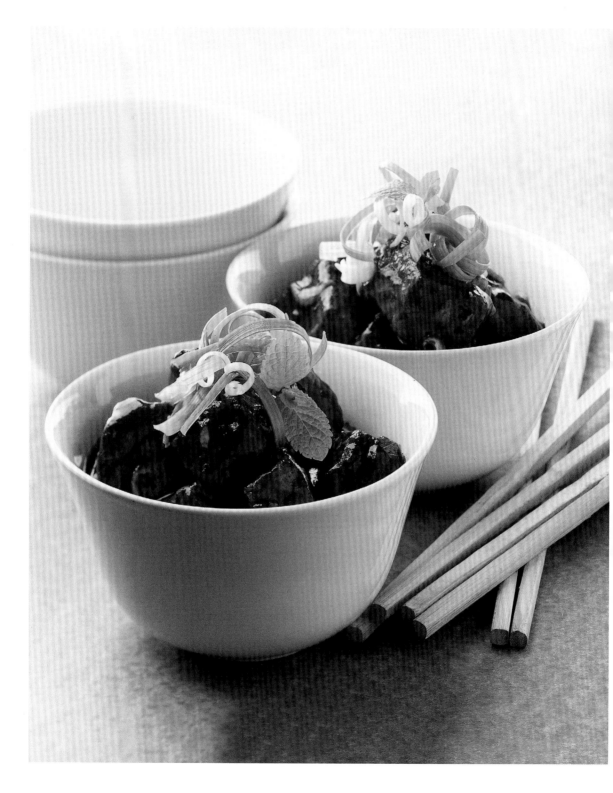

Vietnamese beef

1 lemon grass stalk, peeled and chopped

a few fresh mint leaves, chopped

3 tablespoons Thai fish sauce

1 teaspoon brown sugar

2.5-cm/1-inch piece of fresh ginger, peeled and grated

1 fresh red chilli/chile, seeded and finely chopped

2 garlic cloves, crushed

freshly ground black pepper

1 kg/2¼ lbs. boneless beef (shin/ foreshank or chuck), cut into 2.5-cm/1-inch cubes

4 tablespoons groundnut/peanut oil

2 tablespoons tomato purée/paste

400-g/14-oz. can chopped tomatoes

250 ml/1 cup beef stock

to serve

6 spring onions/scallions, shredded

4–6 sprigs of fresh mint

crusty baguettes

SERVES 4–6

This beef casserole is eaten as street food or at home in Vietnam and is served with crusty baguettes rather than rice, a legacy of the French colonial period. Note that this recipe requires marinating for a minimum of 2 hours before it can be cooked.

Put the lemon grass, mint, fish sauce, sugar, ginger, chilli/chile, garlic and lots of freshly ground black pepper in a bowl and mix well. Add the beef and turn to coat. Cover and marinate in the refrigerator for at least 2 hours or preferably overnight.

Heat the oil in a frying pan/skillet then add the beef in batches and sauté until browned on all sides. Using a slotted spoon, remove each batch to a plate and keep it warm while you cook the remainder.

Return all the beef to the frying pan/skillet, add the tomato purée/ paste and tomatoes, and cook for 1–2 minutes. Add the stock and bring to the boil. Transfer to the slow cooker, cover with the lid and cook on HIGH for 4 hours until the meat is tender.

Serve topped with shredded spring onions/scallions and mint sprigs, accompanied by crusty baguettes for mopping up the juices.

braised pork chops with tomato, orange & chilli/chili

The flavours in this dish point straight to Spain, though it is not traditional. This dish cries out for slow cooking, as the flavours need time to mingle and develop. It's a very homey sort of food, perfect with potatoes, preferably mashed or sautéed, and some green beans on the side.

2 tablespoons olive oil

8 bone-in pork chops, about 280 g/ 10 oz. each, trimmed

3 celery stalks, chopped

1 onion, chopped

4 garlic cloves, finely chopped

½–1 teaspoon dried red chilli/hot pepper flakes

125 ml/½ cup full-bodied red wine, preferably Rioja

freshly squeezed juice of 1 orange, orange reserved

400-g/14-oz. can chopped tomatoes

1 fresh or dried bay leaf

a few sprigs of fresh oregano

sea salt

to serve
mashed potatoes (optional)

green beans (optional)

SERVES 4–6

Heat the oil in a large frying pan/skillet. Add the pork chops and cook for 3–5 minutes until browned. Turn and cook the other side (work in batches if they don't all fit in the frying pan/skillet). Transfer to the slow cooker and season with salt.

Arrange the celery, onion, garlic and chilli/pepper flakes on top of the chops. Pour the wine into the frying pan/skillet and stir, scraping any bits that are stuck to the bottom of the frying pan/ skillet. Pour over the pork and vegetables along with the orange juice and add the tomatoes, bay leaf, oregano and salt to taste. Quarter the orange used for the juice and tuck 1 piece into the sauce. Cover with the lid. Cook on HIGH for 5–6 hours until the pork is tender, turning the meat halfway through cooking.

Remove and discard the orange piece, bay leaf and herbs. Serve the chops with the sauce spooned over the top. Mashed potatoes and green beans make a good accompaniment.

Portuguese lamb stew with piri piri

1 kg/2¼ lbs. boneless lamb, cubed

2 tablespoons olive oil

3 tablespoons plain/all-purpose flour

675 ml/2¾ cups lamb stock

400-g/14-oz. can chickpeas, drained

500 g/1 lb. 2 oz. potatoes, peeled and cut into large chunks

500 g/1 lb. 2 oz. carrots, cut into large pieces

1 red (bell) pepper, seeded and cut into pieces

1 courgette/zucchini, cut into thick slices

1–2 teaspoons hot piri piri sauce

sea salt and freshly ground black pepper

couscous, to serve

marinade

1 onion, chopped

6 tablespoons sherry vinegar

1½ teaspoons Spanish smoked sweet paprika (pimentón dulce)

4 garlic cloves, sliced

a large handful of chopped fresh coriander/cilantro

a large handful of chopped fresh flat-leaf parsley

1 tablespoon sea salt

SERVES 6

This spicy stew makes a nice change from the standard repertoire. The heat comes from Portuguese piri piri sauce, which is very hot and can vary from one brand to another, so be cautious if you've not tried it before – you can always add more sauce later if it's not hot enough. Note this recipe requires marinating for at least 3 hours before cooking.

To make the marinade, put the onion, vinegar, paprika, garlic, coriander/cilantro, parsley and salt in a large non-reactive dish. Mix well, then add the lamb and turn to coat thoroughly. Cover with clingfilm/plastic wrap and refrigerate for at least 3 hours or overnight.

Heat the oil in a large saucepan. When hot, add the lamb and all the marinade. Cook for 5–8 minutes until the lamb is well sealed. Sprinkle with the flour, stir to coat well and cook for 1–2 minutes. Pour in the stock and chickpeas, stir well and bring to the boil.

Put the potatoes and carrots in the bottom of the slow cooker. Spoon over the lamb, stock and chickpea mixture (not stirring into vegetables underneath) then cover with the lid and cook on HIGH for 4 hours. Remove the lid, add the (bell) pepper, courgette/zucchini, piri piri and seasoning, cover and cook for 1 further hour.

Remove the lid, stir well and, if the sauce is a little watery, simmer for a further 10–15 minutes with the lid off. Adjust the seasoning to taste and serve with couscous.

meatballs in red (bell) pepper sauce

50 g/1 cup fresh breadcrumbs

3 tablespoons milk

1 small onion, finely chopped

a handful of fresh flat-leaf parsley leaves, chopped

2 garlic cloves, crushed

800 g/1¾ cups minced/ground meat, preferably a mix of beef and pork

1½ teaspoons fine sea salt

1 teaspoon dried oregano

1 teaspoon ground cumin

½ teaspoon paprika

1 egg, beaten

red pepper sauce

a few sprigs of fresh thyme

1 fresh or dried bay leaf

2 tablespoons olive oil

1 onion, grated

6 garlic cloves, crushed

¼ teaspoon cayenne pepper

5 tablespoons red wine

½ unwaxed orange, well scrubbed

1 litre/4 cups passata (Italian strained tomatoes)

½ large jar roasted red (bell) peppers, drained and chopped

sea salt and freshly ground black pepper

kitchen string/twine

MAKES ABOUT 25 MEATBALLS

This is great family food, best served with sautéed potatoes. Should you have any leftover, it makes a great sandwich filling. If you don't have time to make the sauce, substitute prepared pasta sauce for speed (you'll need two 450-g/1-lb. jars).

To make the red (bell) pepper sauce, tie up the thyme and bay leaf with kitchen string/twine. Heat the oil in a frying pan/skillet. Add the onion and a pinch of salt and cook for 2–3 minutes until soft. Add the garlic and cayenne and cook, stirring, for 1 minute. Stir in the wine and squeeze in the orange juice (reserve the rest of the orange) and cook for 30 seconds. Add the passata, a good pinch of salt, the bunch of herbs and the reserved orange. Simmer gently for 20–30 minutes until thick. Season to taste with salt and pepper. Stir in the red (bell) peppers, remove the herbs and orange and leave the sauce until needed. It can be made a day ahead and stored covered in the refrigerator, if needed.

To make the meatballs, put the breadcrumbs, milk, onion, parsley, garlic, minced/ground meat, salt, oregano, cumin, paprika and beaten egg in a large bowl. Mix well (your hands are best). Shape spoonfuls of the meat mixture into balls, just slightly larger than a golf ball.

Put the meatballs in the slow cooker, pour over the (reheated) sauce and gently stir to coat the meatballs, taking care not to break them. Cover with the lid and cook on HIGH for 2 hours. Shake the cooker from time to time to keep the meatballs separate.

sausage & butter/lima bean stew

*This is a cheat's version of a Spanish peasant stew called a fabada –
beans, sausage and a rich tomato and red wine sauce make a welcoming
supper to come home to on a cold winter's evening. If you can't get hold
of chorizo, any spicy sausage will do.*

2 tablespoons olive oil

2 onions, finely chopped

4 garlic cloves, crushed

200 g/7 oz. chorizo sausage, skin
removed and cut into 1-cm/½-inch
slices

200 ml/¾ cup red wine

3 x 400-g/14-oz. cans chopped
tomatoes

2 red onions, cut into thin petals

3 x 400-g/14-oz. cans butter/lima beans,
drained

2 teaspoon dried mixed herbs

a few sprigs of fresh rosemary
or thyme

sea salt and freshly ground
black pepper

4 tablespoons freshly grated Parmesan
cheese (optional)

warm crusty bread, to serve (optional)

SERVES 6

Heat the oil in a large, high-sided frying pan/skillet. Add the onions
and garlic and cook for a few minutes over medium heat. Add the
chorizo sausage and cook for a further 2–3 minutes. Add the red
wine and bring to the boil.

Transfer to the slow cooker, adding the tomatoes, red onion petals,
butter/lima beans, 100 ml/scant ½ cup water, the dried mixed herbs
and rosemary or thyme sprigs.

Cover with the lid and cook on HIGH for 2 hours.

Season to taste with salt and pepper and spoon into warmed
serving bowls. Sprinkle with the Parmesan cheese, if using, and
serve immediately with chunks of warm crusty bread to mop up
the rich juices.

lamb rogan josh

This slow-cooked lamb stew from Kashmir in north India is perfect for hassle-free entertaining as it almost cooks itself!

2 tablespoons safflower oil

800 g/1¾ lbs. boneless lamb shoulder, cut into large bite-size pieces

2 large onions, thickly sliced

3 garlic cloves, crushed

2 teaspoons finely grated fresh ginger

2 cinnamon sticks

2 teaspoons chilli/chili powder

2 teaspoons paprika

6 cardamom pods

4 tablespoons medium curry paste

400-g/14-oz. can chopped tomatoes

6 tablespoons tomato purée/paste

1 teaspoon sugar

150 ml/⅔ cup lamb stock

4–6 potatoes, peeled and left whole

a handful of chopped fresh coriander/cilantro, to garnish

plain yogurt, to serve

SERVES 4

Heat 1 tablespoon of the safflower oil in a large casserole dish or heavy-based saucepan. Add the lamb in batches and cook for 3–4 minutes until evenly browned. Remove with a slotted spoon and transfer to the slow cooker.

Add the remaining oil to the casserole and add the onions. Cook over medium heat for 10–12 minutes, stirring often, until soft and lightly browned. Add the garlic, ginger, cinnamon, chilli/chili powder, paprika and cardamom pods. Stir-fry for 1–2 minutes, then add the curry paste. Stir-fry for 2–3 minutes, then stir in the canned tomatoes, tomato purée/paste, sugar, stock and potatoes. Season well, bring to the boil, and pour over the lamb in the slow cooker. Cook on HIGH for 7–8 hours.

To serve, sprinkle with the chopped coriander/cilantro and drizzle with yogurt.

beef & pea curry

Minced/ground beef is cooked slowly with spices and peas resulting in a subtle, fragrant curry which is great accompanied by steamed basmati rice or bread.

2 tablespoons safflower oil

1 large onion, finely chopped

3 garlic cloves, crushed

1 teaspoon finely grated fresh ginger

2 fresh green chillies/chiles, seeded and thinly sliced

1 tablespoon cumin seeds

4 tablespoons medium curry paste

800 g/1¾ lbs. minced/ground beef

400-g/14-oz. can chopped tomatoes

1 teaspoon sugar

4 tablespoons tomato purée/paste

4 tablespoons coconut cream

250 g/9 oz. frozen peas, defrosted

sea salt and freshly ground black pepper

a handful of chopped fresh coriander/cilantro, to garnish

steamed basmati rice, to serve

SERVES 4

Heat the safflower oil in a large heavy-based saucepan and add the onion. Cook over low heat for 15 minutes until softened and just turning light golden.

Add the garlic, ginger, chillies/chiles, cumin seeds and curry paste and stir-fry over high heat for 1–2 minutes. Add the minced/ground beef and stir-fry for 3–4 minutes until the meat is browned, then stir in the canned tomatoes, sugar, tomato purée/paste and 100 ml/scant ½ cup cold water and bring to the boil. Transfer to the slow cooker, season, cover with the lid, and cook on HIGH for 5 hours. Stir in the coconut cream and peas 1 hour before the end of cooking time.

Sprinkle with the chopped coriander/cilantro and serve with steamed basmati rice.

beef madras

800 g/1¾ lbs. stewing beef, cut into large bite-size pieces

2 tablespoons safflower oil

1 large onion, thinly sliced

3 garlic cloves, crushed

1 tablespoon finely grated fresh ginger

1 teaspoon ground turmeric

1 fresh red chilli/chile, split in half lengthways

2 teaspoons hot chilli/chili powder

2 teaspoons ground cumin

200-g/7-oz. can chopped tomatoes

300 g/1¼ cups coconut milk, plus extra to drizzle

¼ teaspoon garam masala

sea salt and freshly ground black pepper

a small handful of chopped fresh coriander/cilantro, to garnish

steamed basmati rice and poppadoms, to serve

marinade

5 tablespoons plain yogurt (not low fat)

3 tablespoons Madras curry paste

SERVES 4

This fiery curry from southern India is not for the faint-hearted, although you can decrease the amounts of chilli/chile and curry powder to suit your palate. Serve with poppadoms, as well as steamed basmati rice.

To make the marinade, combine the yogurt and curry paste in a glass bowl. Stir in the beef, season with salt, cover and let marinate in the fridge for at least 30 minutes.

Heat the safflower oil in a large non-stick frying pan/skillet and add the onion. Stir-fry over medium heat for 4–5 minutes, then add the garlic, ginger, turmeric, red chilli/chile, chilli/chili powder and cumin. Add the marinated beef and stir-fry for 5 minutes until the meat is sealed.

Transfer the meat mixture to the slow cooker and add the canned tomatoes. Cover with the lid and cook on HIGH for 7 hours.

Stir in the coconut milk and garam masala 5 minutes before the end of the cooking time. Season to taste, drizzle with coconut milk and garnish with the chopped coriander/cilantro. Serve with steamed basmati rice and poppadoms.

lamb & broad/fava bean tagine

A tagine is a Moroccan stew that's traditionally cooked in a large-lidded terracotta pot, which gives the dish its name. Like all stews made with aromatic spices, this tastes even better the next day, once the flavours have mingled, so it's perfect for cooking the day before – simply reheat when you are ready to serve the following evening.

1.25 kg/2¾ lbs. boneless shoulder of lamb or shoulder chops, cut into large chunks

2 teaspoons ground cinnamon

2 teaspoons ground cumin

½ teaspoon hot chilli/chili powder

1 teaspoon ground turmeric

a pinch of saffron threads

½ teaspoon ground white pepper

4 tablespoons olive oil

3 onions, chopped

3 garlic cloves, crushed

400 ml/1½ cups hot lamb or vegetable stock

200 g/1 cup broad/fava beans, podded

150 g/1 cup dates, pitted

a handful of chopped fresh coriander/cilantro, to garnish

couscous, to serve

SERVES 4

Put the lamb in a large bowl and toss with the cinnamon, cumin, chilli/chili powder, turmeric, saffron and pepper.

Heat 2 tablespoons of the olive oil in a frying pan/skillet set over medium heat, then add half the lamb. Cook for 2–3 minutes, stirring occasionally, until the lamb is evenly browned. Tip into a bowl, add more oil to the pan and brown the remainder of the lamb. Remove and then add the onions and garlic. Stir-fry for a few minutes until softened. Return the lamb to the pan and add the stock and a large pinch of salt. Bring the mixture to the boil, then transfer it to the slow cooker.

Cover with the lid and cook on HIGH for 1 hour then stir in the broad/fava beans. Cook on HIGH for 1 further hour before adding the dates, then cook on HIGH for 1–2 hours, until the meat is so tender that it falls apart easily.

Sprinkle over the coriander/cilantro and serve with couscous.

lamb & butternut squash stew

This is a deliciously different stew that is very simple to make but tastes quite exotic. Serve with plenty of buttery couscous and a crispy salad.

800 g/1¾ lbs. stewing lamb, cubed

3 tablespoons plain/all-purpose flour seasoned with salt and pepper

1 teaspoon cumin seeds

1 teaspoon fennel seeds

6 tablespoons olive oil

1 onion, chopped

1 small butternut squash, peeled, seeded and cubed

400 ml/1½ cups lamb or vegetable stock

a pinch of saffron threads

1 cinnamon stick

1 whole garlic bulb, separated

a handful of fresh coriander/cilantro, to garnish

couscous, to serve

SERVES 4

Place the lamb in a plastic bag with the seasoned flour and shake to coat well.

Toast the cumin and fennel seeds for 1–2 minutes in a small dry frying pan/skillet set over medium heat until fragrant.

Heat 4 tablespoons of the oil in a large casserole dish or heavy-based saucepan. Add the lamb in batches and fry until brown all over, then remove from the frying pan/skillet. Add the remaining oil and fry the onion for 2–3 minutes until soft. Add the butternut squash and cook for 3–4 minutes. Return the lamb to the pan and pour in the stock. Add the toasted spices, saffron, cinnamon and separated garlic cloves (there is no need to peel them). Bring to the boil, then transfer to the slow cooker. Cook on HIGH for 3–4 hours until the lamb is tender.

Sprinkle over the coriander/cilantro and serve with couscous.

Tip: Do try squeezing the softened garlic out of its skin and smearing it on the tender chunks of lamb.

lamb shanks with red wine, rosemary & garlic

6 even-size lamb shanks, about 2 kg/4½ lbs. in total

1 large onion, thinly sliced

3 carrots, cut into thin batons

4 garlic cloves, thinly sliced

2–3 sprigs of fresh rosemary

½ teaspoon black peppercorns

500 ml/2 cups red wine, such as Shiraz, Malbec or Zinfandel

4 tablespoons olive oil

500 ml/2 cups passata (Italian strained tomatoes)

tomato ketchup, to taste

sea salt and freshly ground black pepper

creamy mashed potatoes, to serve

a large, strong plastic bag

SERVES 6

Believe it or not, the preparation and cooking of this dish can be spread over three days, which makes it the perfect dish to serve for Sunday lunch. Start marinating the meat on Friday evening, cook it on Saturday, then simply reheat it on Sunday.

Put the lamb shanks in the large, strong plastic bag. Add the onion, carrots, garlic, rosemary and peppercorns. Pour in the bottle of wine, then pull up the sides of the bag so the marinade covers the meat. Secure the top of the bag with a wire twist. Put the bag in a bowl or dish and refrigerate overnight.

The next day, remove the lamb shanks from the marinade, pat them dry with paper towels and season with salt and pepper. Reserve the vegetables and marinade.

Heat half of the oil in a large flameproof casserole dish, add the lamb shanks and brown them thoroughly on all sides – you may need to do this in batches. Transfer the lamb shanks to the slow cooker. Add the remaining oil to the casserole dish, then add the reserved vegetables and fry briefly until they begin to soften. Add the reserved marinade and bubble for about 5 minutes, incorporating any caramelized juices that have stuck to the casserole dish. Stir in the passata, then pour over the lamb shanks in the slow cooker. Cook on HIGH for 7–8 hours.

Skim off any fat from the surface of the sauce then season to taste with salt and pepper and sweeten with a little tomato ketchup, if necessary. Serve with creamy mashed potatoes.

lamb kefta meatballs

If you are interested in cooking with spices, Moroccan food is a great place to start. This style of cooking uses a relatively short list of staple spices, such as cumin, cinnamon and cayenne pepper, but they are all used in varying quantities to produce very different results from one recipe to the next.

500 g/1 lb. 2 oz. minced/ground lamb

1 large onion, grated or very finely chopped

2 garlic cloves, finely chopped

a handful of fresh flat-leaf parsley leaves, finely chopped

beaten egg, to bind

plain/all-purpose flour, to dust

4 tablespoons olive oil

1 teaspoon ground cumin

1 teaspoon ground cinnamon

400-g/14-oz. can chopped tomatoes

½ teaspoon cayenne pepper

a large handful of chopped fresh coriander/cilantro, to garnish

crunchy salad and pita bread, to serve

SERVES 4

Put the lamb, half of the onion, half of the garlic and all the parsley in a bowl and add a little beaten egg to bind. Use your hands to combine and throw the mixture against the side of the bowl several times. Then, using lightly floured hands, divide the mixture into approximately 24 walnut-size balls. Toss each in a little flour to lightly coat, cover and chill in the fridge.

Heat half of the oil in a large, heavy-based frying pan/skillet set over high heat. Add the remaining onion and garlic and cook for 3–4 minutes until softened and golden. Add the spices and cook, stirring constantly, for 1 minute until aromatic. Add the tomatoes and 250 ml/1 cup water and bring to the boil. Transfer the tomato sauce to the slow cooker.

Heat the remaining olive oil in a large frying pan/skillet set over medium heat. Add the meatballs and fry for 3–5 minutes, turning frequently until well browned. Transfer the meatballs to the tomato sauce in the slow cooker, cover with the lid, and cook on HIGH for 3 hours. Stir in the cayenne pepper and cook for 1 hour further. (Cayenne can become bitter if cooked for too long a time.)

Sprinkle over the coriander/cilantro and serve with crunchy salad and pita bread.

rich Bolognese sauce

Like many classic, handed-down recipes, there are countless versions of Bolognese sauce. Some Italian chefs add sweetbreads, chicken livers and veal, but here this homey recipe uses a mixture of minced/ground beef and Parma ham. It really benefits from being chilled overnight, so it's ideal for making the day before; gently reheat when you are ready to serve.

15 g/½ oz. dried porcini mushrooms, rinsed

1 tablespoon olive oil

1 onion, finely chopped

450 g/1 lb. minced/ground beef

50 g/2 oz. Parma ham or prosciutto, coarsely chopped

80 ml/⅓ cup Marsala or sherry

680 ml/2¾ cups passata (Italian strained tomatoes)

sea salt and freshly ground black pepper

spaghetti or linguine, to serve

shavings of fresh Parmesan cheese, to serve

SERVES 4

Put the porcini into a bowl, cover with boiling water and set aside for 20 minutes until softened.

Heat the oil in a large saucepan, add the onion and cook for 2 minutes. Add the beef and Parma ham and cook for about 3–4 minutes, stirring, until evenly browned.

Drain the porcini and discard the soaking water. Chop the porcini, then add to the pan with the Marsala and passata. Bring to the boil and transfer to the slow cooker. Cover with the lid and cook on HIGH for 4 hours. Remove the lid for the last 30 minutes of cooking time to reduce and thicken the sauce. Add salt and pepper to taste.

Cook the pasta according to the package instructions. Drain well and divide between serving plates or bowls. Top with the Bolognese sauce and add some extra black pepper and some fresh Parmesan shavings, to serve.

chunky diner-style chili

1 kg/2¼ lbs. braising steak, cut into 4-cm/1½-inch chunks

500 ml/2 cups beer

2 tablespoons olive oil

2 large onions, roughly chopped

6 garlic cloves, finely chopped

1 fresh red chilli/chile, seeded and finely chopped

2 x 400-g/14-oz. cans chopped tomatoes

3 tablespoons cider vinegar

1 tablespoon brown sugar

1 tablespoon Spanish smoked sweet paprika (pimentón dulce)

1 tablespoon mild chilli/chili powder

2 tablespoons ground cumin

400-g/14-oz. can kidney, borlotti or pinto beans, drained and rinsed

sea salt and freshly ground black pepper

to serve

boiled white rice

chopped red onion

grated cheese

a handful of fresh coriander/cilantro

crackers (optional)

SERVES 4–6

A chunky chili con carne is a diner institution, traditionally served with little cellophane packages of saltine crackers. Chunks of tender steak and puréed dried chillies/chiles make this mouth-watering version a bit more special.

Put the beef in a bowl, pour the beer over and let marinate for 30 minutes. Drain, reserving 150 ml/⅔ cup of the liquid and pat the beef dry with paper towels.

In a large saucepan, heat 1 tablespoon of the olive oil. Season the meat and sear in batches until evenly browned. Remove from the pan and set aside. Add the remaining olive oil and sauté the onions, garlic and chilli/chile for 5 minutes.

Put the meat and onion mixture into the slow cooker. Add the chopped tomatoes, cider vinegar, brown sugar, paprika, chilli/chili powder and cumin and season well. Cover with the lid and cook on HIGH for 6 hours, adding the beans 1 hour before the end of cooking time just to warm them through.

Serve in small bowls with cooked rice, chopped red onion, grated cheese, coriander/cilantro or crackers, if liked.

Mexican pork & beans
in red chilli/chile sauce

1 onion, roughly chopped

4 garlic cloves, roughly chopped

1 red (bell) pepper, halved, seeded and roughly chopped

1 fresh red chilli/chile, seeded and chopped

2 teaspoons mild chilli/chili powder

1 teaspoon sweet paprika

1 teaspoon ground cumin

1 teaspoon ground coriander

½ teaspoon ground cinnamon

1 teaspoon dried oregano

150 ml/⅔ cup lager beer

500 g/1 lb. 2 oz. pork steaks

4 tablespoons safflower oil

200-g/7-oz. can chopped tomatoes

150 ml/⅔ cup tomato juice or passata (Italian strained tomatoes)

25 g/1 oz. very dark chocolate, chopped, or ½ tablespoon unsweetened cocoa powder

400-g/14-oz. can pinto beans or black-eyed beans/peas, drained and rinsed

sea salt and freshly ground black pepper

to serve

fresh tomato and red onion salsa

chopped avocado

sour cream

soft flour tortillas or rice

SERVES 4–6

This version of chili is not too spicy, made with pork, not beef, and just a few beans, then enriched Mexican-style with a little chocolate for depth. Serve it with generous bowls of a simple fresh tomato and red onion salsa, chopped avocado, sour cream, a pile of warmed soft tortillas or a big bowl of rice for a great family feast.

Put the onion, garlic, red (bell) pepper, chilli/chile, chilli/chili powder, paprika, cumin, coriander, cinnamon and oregano in a food processor. Add half the lager and blend to a smooth purée.

Trim the pork steaks, then cut into large pieces. Working in batches, heat the oil in a large frying pan/skillet, add the pork and fry until browned. Transfer to a plate.

Add the purée to the pan and cook, stirring continuously, over moderate heat for 5 minutes – make sure it doesn't catch and burn, but it should start to caramelize. Stir in the tomatoes, tomato juice, pork and the juices. Season with salt and pepper and bring to the boil. Transfer to the slow cooker, cover with the lid and cook on HIGH for 2 hours. Stir in the chocolate and beans and cook for 1 further hour.

Serve with the accompaniments of your choice.

Burmese pork hinleh

3 tablespoons groundnut/peanut or vegetable oil

750 g/1½ lbs. well trimmed boneless pork sparerib, sliced into chunks

350 ml/1½ cups beef stock

curry paste (hinleh)

4–6 fresh red bird's eye chillies/chiles, seeded and chopped

5 garlic cloves, quartered

½ onion, roughly chopped

5-cm/2-inch piece of fresh ginger, peeled and grated

¼ teaspoon ground turmeric

5-cm/2-inch piece of fresh galangal, peeled and grated

1 lemon grass stalk, outer leaves discarded, the remainder very finely chopped

3 anchovies in oil, drained and finely chopped

1 tablespoon Thai fish sauce

to serve

a handful of chopped fresh coriander/cilantro

2 fresh red bird's eye chillies/chiles, finely sliced lengthways

basmati rice

SERVES 4

This curry is a Burmese speciality and doesn't include coconut milk (so typical of South-east Asian cooking), which makes it more suitable for preparing in a slow cooker. Boneless sparerib meat gives the best results at a lower temperature, so do look out for it. If you can't get fresh galangal, use extra fresh ginger instead.

To make the curry paste, put all the ingredients in a small food processor and blend to a paste, adding a dash of water to help the blades run.

Heat the oil in a large saucepan and add the curry paste. Stir-fry for 5 minutes. Add the pork and stir-fry to seal.

Transfer the pork to the slow cooker, add the stock, cover with the lid, and cook on HIGH for 7 hours until very tender. Sprinkle with the coriander/cilantro and chilli/chile and serve with rice.

beef & carrot casserole
with cheese dumplings

Think of chilly, dark evenings and this is exactly what you'd want to eat.
The feather-light dumplings nestling in the rich, savoury casserole will
have everyone asking for second helpings.

800 g/1¾ lbs. chuck steak, cut into cubes

2 tablespoons plain/all-purpose flour seasoned with salt and pepper

4 tablespoons olive oil

1 onion, chopped

2 garlic cloves, crushed

2 celery stalks, chopped

4 carrots, chopped

300 ml/1¼ cups beef stock

150 ml/⅔ cup red wine

2 dried bay leaves

sea salt and freshly ground black pepper

a handful of chopped fresh flat-leaf parsley, to garnish

cheese dumplings

1 teaspoon baking powder

200 g/1⅔ cups plain/all-purpose flour

75 g/3 oz. solid vegetable shortening, such as Trex/Crisco

75 g/3 oz. mature/sharp Cheddar cheese, grated

SERVES 4–6

Place the beef in a strong plastic bag with the seasoned flour and shake to coat well.

Heat 3 tablespoons of the oil in a large frying pan/skillet. Add the beef and fry in batches until brown all over, then remove from the frying pan/skillet. Add the remaining oil and fry the onion, garlic, celery and carrots for 2–3 minutes until soft. Add the stock, red wine, seasoning and bay leaves. Bring to the boil, then transfer to the slow cooker. Cover with the lid and cook on HIGH for 2–3 hours.

To make the dumplings, put the flour and baking powder in a bowl and rub in the vegetable fat until it resembles breadcrumbs. Add the cheese, mixing it in with a knife. Add 75–100 ml/⅓ cup of cold water and use your hands to bring the mixture together and form a dough. Divide the dough into 8 pieces of equal size and roll them into balls.

Place the dumplings on top of the casserole, re-cover with the lid, and cook on HIGH for 1 further hour. Serve sprinkled with parsley.

POULTRY

chicken & bacon pot

*The bacon adds a special intensity to the flavour of this easy-to-make dish.
It crisps up better if dry-fried before adding to the slow cooker as this
allows the fat to render out. Serve with rice to mop up the lovely sauce.
The dish is already quite salty because of the bacon, so add salt sparingly.*

300 g/10 oz. thick bacon, chopped

250 g/9 oz. button mushrooms

4 skinless chicken breasts

1 tablespoon olive oil

1 tablespoon butter

1 garlic clove, crushed

2 shallots, chopped

3 tablespoons plain/all-purpose flour

500 ml/2 cups chicken stock

200 ml/¾ cup white wine

1 fresh or dried bay leaf

sea salt and freshly ground
black pepper

a handful of chopped fresh flat-leaf
parsley, to garnish

rice, to serve

SERVES 4

Heat a heavy-based frying pan/skillet, then add the bacon and dry-fry for 3–5 minutes until crisp and golden. Add the mushrooms and cook for 1 further minute. Using a slotted spoon, transfer to a plate.

Add the chicken to the frying pan/skillet and pan-fry for about 3–5 minutes, until browned on both sides. Set aside with the bacon.

Heat the olive oil and butter in the frying pan/skillet, then fry the garlic and shallots over low heat for 2–3 minutes. Add the flour and mix well, then slowly pour in the stock and wine and stir until smooth. Add the bay leaf and season to taste.

Place the chicken breasts in the base of the slow cooker and scatter over the mushrooms and bacon. Pour over the sauce, cover with the lid and cook on HIGH for 3–4 hours.

Sprinkle with the chopped parsley and serve with rice.

coq au vin

This classic French recipe is a great dish for a slow cooker. Serve with plenty of mashed potatoes.

6 large skinless chicken breasts

2 tablespoons plain/all-purpose flour, seasoned with salt and pepper, plus 1 tablespoon extra for the sauce (optional)

3 tablespoons olive oil

125 g/4 oz. chopped streaky/fatty bacon or pancetta cubes

300 g/10 oz. shallots, left whole if small or halved or quartered if larger

2 garlic cloves, thinly sliced

3 tablespoons brandy

3 sprigs of fresh thyme

1 dried bay leaf

750-ml bottle dry, fruity red wine

250 g/9 oz. small button mushrooms

1 tablespoon butter, softened (optional)

sea salt and freshly ground black pepper

a handful of chopped fresh flat-leaf parsley, to garnish

creamy mashed potatoes, to serve

SERVES 6

Dip the chicken breasts in the seasoned flour and coat both sides. Heat 2 tablespoons of the olive oil in a large frying pan/skillet, add the chicken breasts and fry for 2–3 minutes on each side, until lightly browned – you may have to do this in batches.

Remove the chicken from the frying pan/skillet, discard the oil and wipe the pan with a paper towel. Return the frying pan/skillet to the heat and add the remaining oil. Add the bacon and shallots and fry until lightly browned. Stir in the garlic, then return the chicken to the pan. Put the brandy in a small saucepan and heat it until almost boiling. Set it alight with a long kitchen match and carefully pour it over the chicken. Let the flames die down, then add the thyme and bay leaf, and pour in enough wine to cover the chicken. Bring back to simmering point, then transfer to the slow cooker. Cover with the lid and cook on HIGH for 4 hours. After 2 hours, stir in the mushrooms.

If you want to thicken the sauce before serving, remove the chicken from the slow cooker, set aside and keep it warm. Using a slotted spoon, scoop the shallots, bacon pieces and mushrooms out of the slow cooker and keep them warm. Transfer the sauce to a saucepan, increase the heat under the pan and let the sauce simmer until it has reduced by half. Mash 1 tablespoon butter with 1 tablespoon flour to give a smooth roux, then add it bit by bit to the sauce, whisking well after each addition, until the sauce is smooth and glossy. Season to taste.

Cut each chicken breast into 4 slices and arrange them on serving plates. Spoon a generous amount of sauce over the chicken and sprinkle with parsley. Serve with creamy mashed potatoes.

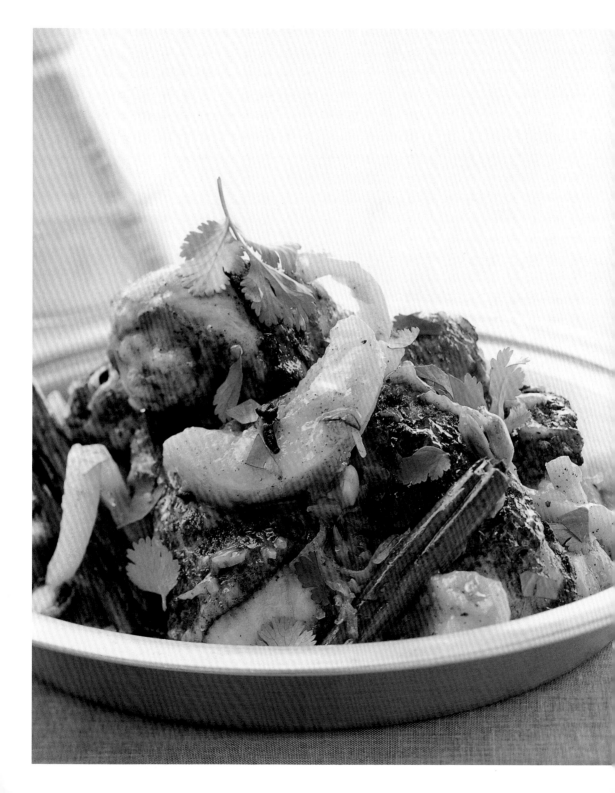

chicken tagine with quinces & preserved lemons

1 teaspoon ground saffron

2.5-cm/1-inch piece of fresh ginger, peeled and grated, or 1 teaspoon ground ginger

1½ tablespoons paprika

1 teaspoon freshly ground black pepper

2 teaspoons ground cinnamon

1 chicken, cut into 8 pieces, skinned

125 ml/½ cup olive oil

2 large onions, grated

a pinch of saffron threads, soaked in boiling water for 30 minutes

6 garlic cloves, crushed

2 cinnamon sticks, broken in half

6 cloves

10 cardamom pods, lightly crushed

2 quinces or slightly unripe pears, cored and cut into wedges

2 preserved lemons (optional)

a handful of fresh coriander/cilantro, to garnish

couscous or rice, to serve

SERVES 4

Tagines often include fruit and quince is a favourite in Morocco but unripe pears can be used instead. Preserved lemons add a salty tang; you can buy them in most larger supermarkets.

Put the ground saffron, ginger, paprika, pepper and ground cinnamon in a bowl and mix well. Rub the chicken pieces in the mixture, put in a bowl, cover with clingfilm/plastic wrap, and marinate for at least 30 minutes or overnight in the refrigerator.

Heat the olive oil in a flame-proof heavy-based casserole dish. Add the chicken pieces and fry on all sides until golden. Add the onions, then the saffron threads and their soaking liquid, the garlic, cinnamon sticks, cloves and cardamom pods.

Add 125 ml/½ cup cold water and bring to the boil. Transfer to the slow cooker. Cover with the lid and cook on LOW for 4 hours.

Peel the quince wedges, add to the tagine, and continue cooking on LOW for 1 further hour until the quinces are tender. If using preserved lemons, cut them in quarters and scrape off and discard the flesh. Cut the zest/peel into thick slices lengthways, stir into the tagine, and heat for about 10 minutes.

Sprinkle with coriander/cilantro leaves and serve with couscous or rice.

chicken & sweet potatoes
with honey, soy & lemon

Sometimes fusions of Western and Eastern ingredients don't work, but this one does, and it's typical of the culinary cross-pollination that happens in Australia and New Zealand. The sweet potato base mops up all the juices from the chicken.

6 tablespoons olive oil

2 sweet potatoes, about 1 kg/2¼ lbs., cut into 1-cm/½-inch rounds

4 skinless chicken legs (thighs and drumsticks)

125 g/1 cup pimento-stuffed green olives

125 ml/½ cup dry white wine

4 tablespoons honey

a large handful of fresh basil, plus extra to garnish

6 garlic cloves, crushed

4 tablespoons light soy sauce

finely grated zest and freshly squeezed juice of 2 lemons, plus lemon wedges to serve

SERVES 4

Heat 4 tablespoons of the oil in a large frying pan/skillet. Add the sweet potatoes and fry until lightly browned. Transfer to the slow cooker and arrange in a layer.

Add the remaining oil to the frying pan/skillet, add the chicken and fry until browned all over. Arrange on top of the sweet potatoes.

Put the olives, wine, honey, basil, garlic, soy sauce, lemon zest and juice in a food processor and purée until smooth. Pour this mixture over the chicken and sweet potatoes in the slow cooker. Cover with the lid and cook on HIGH for 3–4 hours.

Serve with extra basil leaves on top and lemon wedges on the side.

butter chicken

800 g/1¾ lbs. boneless, skinless chicken, cut into bite-size pieces

3 tablespoons butter

1 large onion, finely chopped

1 cinnamon stick

4 cardamom pods

1 teaspoon mild chilli/chili powder

400-g/14-oz. can chopped tomatoes

100 ml/scant ½ cup chicken stock

50 ml/scant ¼ cup single/light cream

sea salt and freshly ground black pepper

a handful of chopped fresh coriander/cilantro, to garnish

basmati rice or naan bread, to serve

marinade

150 g/1 cup cashew nuts

1 tablespoon fennel seeds

2 teaspoons ground cinnamon

1 tablespoon ground coriander

1 teaspoon cardamom seeds, crushed

1 teaspoon black peppercorns

½ teaspoon ground cloves

4 garlic cloves, crushed

2 teaspoons finely grated fresh ginger

2 tablespoons white wine vinegar

6 tablespoons tomato purée/paste

150 g/⅔ cup plain yogurt (not low-fat)

SERVES 4

This popular chicken curry is rich and irresistible. Note that the chicken needs to be marinated in the yogurt mixture overnight. Serve with basmati rice or naan bread for a deliciously different dinner.

To make the marinade, heat a non-stick frying pan/skillet and toast the cashew nuts, fennel seeds, cinnamon, coriander, cardamom seeds, peppercorns and cloves for 2–3 minutes until very aromatic. Transfer to a spice grinder and grind until smooth (or grind with a pestle and mortar).

Add this mixture to a food processor with the garlic, ginger, vinegar, tomato purée/paste and yogurt and process until smooth. Transfer to a large glass bowl. Stir in the chicken pieces, cover with clingfilm/plastic wrap and refrigerate overnight.

Melt the butter in a large frying pan/skillet and add the onion, cinnamon stick and cardamom pods. Stir-fry over medium heat for about 6–8 minutes until the onion has softened. Add the chicken and cook, stirring, for 5 minutes until the chicken is sealed.

Add the chicken mixture to the slow cooker and stir in the chilli/chili powder, canned tomatoes and stock. Cover with the lid and cook on HIGH for 7 hours.

Stir in the cream and season to taste with salt and pepper. Serve immediately, sprinkled with coriander/cilantro and with rice or naan bread on the side.

chicken & lentil curry
with cucumber yogurt

The authentic flavour of this curry comes from using fresh spices and the heady, slightly sour taste of bay leaves. Chicken thigh fillets work better here than breast meat as they are harder to over-cook.

2 tablespoons butter

2 large onions, thinly sliced

2 garlic cloves, crushed

1½ tablespoons garam masala

500 g/1 lb. 2 oz. chicken thigh fillets or breast fillets, cut into chunks

150 g/⅔ cup passata (Italian strained tomatoes)

8 fresh bay or curry leaves

100 g/⅔ cup red lentils

300 ml/1¼ cups chicken or vegetable stock

sea salt and freshly ground black pepper

fresh coriander/cilantro leaves, to garnish

mango chutney and warm chapattis, to serve (optional)

cucumber yogurt

150 ml/⅔ cup plain yogurt

¼ cucumber, cut into ribbons with a potato peeler or chopped

SERVES 4

Melt the butter in a large, lidded frying pan/skillet. Add the onions and stir-fry over medium heat. Once they are sizzling, cover with the lid, reduce the heat, and cook for about 2–3 minutes, stirring occasionally. Add the garlic and garam masala. Cook for a further 3–4 minutes, until the spices start to release their aroma and the onions are beginning to turn golden. Remove the onions from the frying pan/skillet and set aside. Add the chicken to the pan and cook for 5–6 minutes, until browned.

Transfer the chicken and onion mixture to the slow cooker and add the passata, bay leaves, lentils and stock. Cover with the lid and cook on HIGH for 3–4 hours.

Meanwhile, to make the cucumber yogurt, put the yogurt in a bowl, add a good pinch of salt and stir in the cucumber. Cover and set aside in the refrigerator until needed.

When the curry is cooked, season it generously (lentils tend to absorb a lot of seasoning so don't be stingy). Transfer to serving bowls, sprinkle with coriander/cilantro and serve with a dollop of the cucumber yogurt to mix in. Serve with mango chutney and warmed chapattis.

red-cooked chicken legs

Chinese red-cooking involves poaching meat, poultry, game or even fish in a dark, soy-based sauce. When the sauce is spiced with star anise, cinnamon and sometimes additional spices from the five-spice brigade, it is used as a 'master sauce'. Master sauce is used like a stock, cooked first as in the recipe below, then stored for later use (you can freeze it). When it has been used a few times, it is considered mature and more desirable. Serve with rice or noodles.

150 ml/⅔ cup dark soy sauce

3 tablespoons Chinese rice wine or dry sherry

2 thin slices of fresh ginger

3 cinnamon sticks, halved

5 whole star anise

2 whole cloves

3 spring onions/scallions

½ teaspoon finely grated orange or lemon zest

1 tablespoon freshly squeezed lemon juice

½ teaspoon sugar

4 large chicken legs

rice, noodles or stir-fried vegetables, to serve

SERVES 4

Place the soy sauce and rice wine together in a saucepan, then add the ginger, cinnamon, star anise, cloves, spring onions/scallions, orange or lemon zest, lemon juice and sugar. Bring to the boil and turn off the heat. Leave to infuse for at least 10 minutes.

Add the chicken legs and bring to the boil. Transfer to the slow cooker, cover with the lid and cook on HIGH for 3–4 hours.

Transfer the chicken to serving dishes and spoon over some of the sauce. Serve with rice, noodles or stir-fried vegetables.

chicken, sausage & rice

1 fresh or dried bay leaf

a few sprigs of fresh thyme and parsley

1 tablespoon olive oil

8 chicken thighs, trimmed

6 pork sausages

1 onion, chopped

1 red (bell) pepper, seeded and chopped

2 celery stalks, chopped

3 garlic cloves, finely chopped

¼–½ teaspoon dried chilli/hot red pepper flakes, or more to taste

125 ml/½ cup dry wine, red or white

300 ml/1¼ cups chicken or vegetable stock

400-g/14-oz. can chopped tomatoes

370 g/2 cups paella rice, or other short-grain rice

200 g/2 cups peas, fresh or frozen and defrosted

sea salt and freshly ground black pepper

kitchen string/twine

SERVES 4–6

The ingredients here are of the everyday sort but the inspiration for this recipe came from the Spanish dish paella. You can put it together, put it in the slow cooker and forget about it, almost, until serving time. For some reason the dish tastes better if the ingredients aren't packed in too deeply.

Tie the bay leaf, thyme and parsley together with kitchen string/twine.

Heat the oil in a large frying pan/skillet. Add the chicken pieces skin-side down and cook on high for 3–5 minutes on each side until browned. Work in batches if all the pieces will not fit comfortably in the frying pan/skillet. Transfer the browned chicken to a plate and season with salt. Set aside.

Add the sausages to the frying pan/skillet and cook until browned. Remove and cut in 3–4 pieces, depending on their size. Set aside.

Arrange the onion, red (bell) pepper, celery, garlic and chilli/pepper flakes in the slow cooker. Pour in the wine, stock, tomatoes and a pinch of salt and mix well. Add the chicken and sausage and tuck in the herb bundle on the top. Cover with the lid and cook on HIGH for 3 hours.

Add the rice, replace the lid and cook for a further 20 minutes. Put the peas on top and add a little bit of water if the liquid has almost completely evaporated. Cover and cook for a further 10 minutes.

Remove the herb bundle and fluff up the rice to mix in the peas. Serve hot.

pancetta & turkey meatballs

Meatballs are a time-honoured accompaniment to pasta. These delicious little mouthfuls are made with turkey, bacon and herbs, so are somewhat lighter than the traditional all-beef versions.

500 g/1 lb. 2 oz. minced/ground turkey or chicken

50 g/2 oz. thinly sliced pancetta, chopped

6 spring onions/scallions, finely chopped

2 garlic cloves, finely chopped

1–2 fresh red chillies/chiles, seeded and finely chopped (optional)

4 tablespoons freshly grated Parmesan cheese, plus extra to serve

1 tablespoon fresh thyme leaves or 1 teaspoon dried thyme

beaten egg, to bind

plain/all-purpose flour, to dust

2 tablespoons olive oil

175 ml/¾ cup red wine

2 x 400-g/14-oz. cans plum tomatoes

1 tablespoon tomato purée/paste

a pinch of sugar

300 g/10 oz. dried pasta, such as conchiglie

sea salt and freshly ground black pepper

SERVES 4

Put the turkey, pancetta, spring onions/scallions, garlic, chillis/chiles (if using), Parmesan and thyme in a bowl. Add plenty of salt and pepper and just enough beaten egg to bind together, then mix well. Using lightly floured hands, shape into 24 small, firm balls, then roll each in a little flour to coat.

Heat the oil in a large saucepan. Add the meatballs and cook for about 5 minutes, turning frequently until browned all over. Transfer the meatballs to a plate then add the wine to the saucepan and simmer vigorously for 1–2 minutes to deglaze the pan. Add the tomatoes, breaking them up with a wooden spoon. Stir in the tomato purée/paste, sugar and seasoning to taste. Bring to the boil then pour the sauce into the slow cooker. Add the meatballs, cover with the lid and cook on HIGH for 4 hours.

Meanwhile, bring a large saucepan of water to the boil and cook the pasta according to the packet instructions.

Drain the pasta well and return it to the warm pan. Add the meatballs and sauce to the pasta, toss well to mix, then divide between serving bowls. Serve topped with grated Parmesan.

chicken jalfrezi

3 tablespoons vegetable oil

1 onion, roughly chopped

2 garlic cloves, crushed

2 tablespoons hot curry paste

1 tablespoon tomato purée/paste

500 g/1 lb. 2 oz. chicken, cut into bite-size pieces

400-g/14-oz. can chopped tomatoes

1 teaspoon red wine vinegar

100 ml/scant ½ cup chicken stock

125 g/4 oz. chargrilled/broiled red (bell) peppers, chopped

125 g/4 oz. courgette/zucchini, diced

sea salt and freshly ground black pepper

a handful of fresh coriander/cilantro, to garnish

to serve

jasmine rice

poppadoms

SERVES 4

Make sure you have a jar of chargrilled/broiled (bell) peppers for the jalfrezi part and look out for good-quality curry pastes in supermarkets; they cut the time spent grinding or mixing the spices needed for making curry. Go for a hot variety containing spices such as chilli/chili powder, cumin, coriander, tamarind and turmeric. Serve with jasmine rice and poppadoms.

Heat the oil in a large frying pan/skillet. Add the onion and garlic and fry over medium heat for 5 minutes until golden. Add the curry paste and tomato purée/paste and cook for 1 minute. Add the chicken and coat well in the spice mixture. Cook for 5 minutes until the chicken is sealed. Transfer to the slow cooker.

Add the chopped tomatoes, vinegar, chicken stock, chargrilled/broiled red (bell) peppers, courgette/zucchini and seasoning to the slow cooker. Cover with the lid and cook on HIGH for 7 hours.

Garnish with coriander/cilantro and serve with rice and poppadoms.

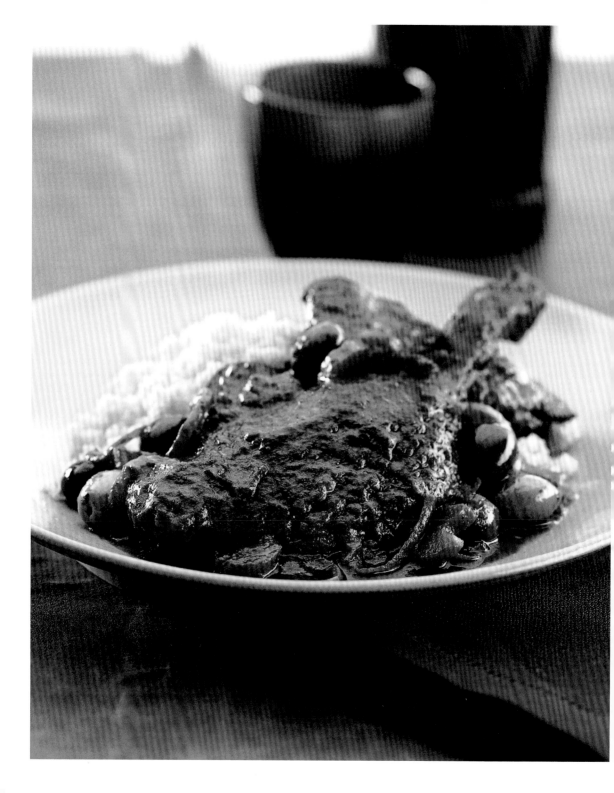

duck casserole with red wine, cinnamon & olives

Red wine and cinnamon are natural partners and work together brilliantly in this spiced casserole. Use a really strong, fruity wine such as a Merlot or Zinfandel.

4 duck legs

2 duck breasts

1 tablespoon olive oil

1 onion, thinly sliced

1 celery stalk, thinly sliced

1 garlic clove, crushed

250 ml/1 cup full-bodied fruity red wine (see recipe introduction), plus 2 tablespoons extra

200 ml/¾ cup passata (Italian strained tomatoes)

2 small strips of orange zest (about 2.5 cm/1 inch wide)

1 cinnamon stick

100 g/⅔ cup pitted mixed olives (marinated with herbs if available)

½ teaspoon herbes de Provence or dried oregano

sea salt and freshly ground black pepper

rice or couscous, to serve

SERVES 4

Preheat the oven to 200°C (400°F) Gas 6.

Trim any excess fat from the duck legs and prick the skin with a fork. Season all the pieces lightly with salt and pepper. Place on a rack set over an ovenproof dish, skin-side upwards. Roast in the preheated oven for 20–25 minutes, then remove from the oven and pour off the fat (keep it for roasting potatoes.)

Meanwhile, heat the oil in a frying pan/skillet. Add the onion and celery and fry over low heat for 5–6 minutes until soft. Stir in the garlic, increase the heat and pour in the red wine. Simmer for about 1–2 minutes, then stir in the passata, orange zest, cinnamon, olives and herbs.

Transfer the duck pieces to the slow cooker and spoon the sauce over them. Cook on HIGH for 3½ hours until the duck is tender.

Discard the cinnamon stick and orange zest and spoon off any fat that has accumulated on the surface. Stir in the 2 tablespoons of red wine and season to taste. Serve with rice or couscous.

chicken & barley braise

This is a simple recipe that makes a lighter alternative to a heavy casserole, so it's perfect for summer eating. The barley adds a good texture and nutty bite, and works very well with the fresh herbs.

2 tablespoons wholemeal/whole-wheat flour

500 g/1 lb. 2 oz. skinless chicken breasts, cut into cubes

100 g/3½ oz. lean bacon slices, cut into strips

2 onions, chopped

2 carrots, sliced

2 celery stalks, chopped

600 ml/2⅓ cups white wine or chicken stock

3 tablespoons pearl barley, rinsed

1 tablespoon mixed chopped fresh herbs, such as rosemary, basil, parsley and thyme

freshly ground black pepper

chopped fresh parsley, to garnish

vegetables of your choice, to serve

SERVES 4

Season the flour with black pepper, then toss the chicken cubes in the flour.

Heat a large, non-stick frying pan/skillet or saucepan, add the bacon and dry-fry for 5 minutes, stirring frequently, until the fat starts to run. Add the chicken and fry for 5–8 minutes, turning often, until the chicken is sealed. Remove the chicken and bacon from the pan with a slotted spoon and put in the slow cooker.

Add the onions, carrots, celery and 4 tablespoons of the wine or stock to the pan and fry for 5 minutes, until the vegetables are softened. Add the pearl barley, herbs and the remaining wine or stock. Bring to the boil and pour the mixture over the chicken in the slow cooker. Cover with the lid and cook on HIGH for 3 hours.

Serve sprinkled with chopped parsley and accompanied by a selection of your favourite vegetables.

bag-cooked chicken with butter/lima beans

4 skinless chicken breasts

10 baby leeks, washed

100 g/3½ oz. baby carrots, halved

400-g/14-oz. can butter/lima beans, drained, rinsed and mashed

100 g/3½ oz. baby corn

100 g/3½ oz. green beans, trimmed

2–3 garlic cloves, sliced

a few sprigs of fresh tarragon, plus extra chopped tarragon, to serve

250 ml/1 cup white wine or chicken stock

1 teaspoon Dijon mustard

150 ml/⅔ cup crème fraîche or sour cream

sea salt and freshly ground black pepper

broccoli, to serve (optional)

2 plastic steaming bags

SERVES 4

This is a light and healthy recipe that uses your slow cooker to slowly steam the ingredients in a bag. Use bags made for microwave or conventional ovens, such as steam cooking bags or roasting bags.

Put 2 chicken breasts in each steaming bag and divide the leeks, carrots, butter beans, corn, green beans, garlic, tarragon and white wine between them. Season with salt and pepper and close loosely with a nylon tie, then place in the slow cooker. Add enough boiling water to the slow cooker to come about 3–4 cm/1½ inches up the bags. Cover with the lid and cook on HIGH for 1½ hours.

Meanwhile, put the mustard and crème fraîche in a bowl and mix together. Use tongs to remove the bags from the slow cooker and open carefully. Transfer the contents to serving plates.

Top with a spoonful of the crème fraîche mixture and sprinkle with extra chopped tarragon. Serve immediately on its own or with your choice of green vegetable, such as broccoli.

spicy chicken curry with squash & spinach

Winter squash such as butternut are great for slow cooking as they retain their shape better than other vegetables. This colourful and delicious curry is best served with fluffy steamed basmati rice.

2 tablespoons safflower or groundnut/peanut oil

1 tablespoon mustard seeds

2 onions, thinly sliced

2 garlic cloves, crushed

2.5-cm/1-inch piece of fresh ginger, peeled and grated (optional)

a pinch of ground turmeric

4 skinless chicken breasts, cut into 2-cm/¾-inch slices

500 g/1 lb. 2 oz. tomatoes, skinned and roughly chopped

500 g/1 lb. 2 oz. winter squash such as butternut or pumpkin, peeled, seeded, and cut into 1-cm/½-inch cubes

150 ml/⅔ cup double/heavy cream

400 g/14 oz. fresh spinach

1 teaspoon garam masala

sea salt and freshly ground black pepper

basmati rice and naan bread, to serve

SERVES 4

Heat the oil in a large non-stick frying pan/skillet or wok. Add the mustard seeds and fry until they pop. Add the onions and stir-fry gently until softened and translucent. Add the garlic and ginger and stir-fry for 1 minute. Add the turmeric and fry for 1 minute more.

Add the chicken, stir-fry until sealed on all sides, then put in the slow cooker along with the tomatoes and squash. Season generously. Cover with the lid and cook on HIGH for 2½ hours.

Stir in the cream, spinach and garam masala and cook for a further 20–30 minutes. Serve with basmati rice and naan bread.

FISH & SEAFOOD

tiger prawn/jumbo shrimp curry

2 tablespoons vegetable oil

1 onion, finely chopped

3 garlic cloves, crushed

5-cm/2-inch piece of fresh ginger, peeled and finely chopped

1 mild fresh red chilli/chile, seeded and chopped

1 teaspoon ground turmeric

2 teaspoons medium curry powder

1 teaspoon ground coriander

1 teaspoon ground cumin

400-g/14-oz. can chopped tomatoes

100 ml/scant ½ cup fish or vegetable stock

freshly squeezed juice of 2 limes

500 g/1 lb. 2 oz. raw peeled tiger prawns/jumbo shrimp, defrosted if frozen

2 tablespoons chopped fresh coriander/cilantro

sea salt and freshly ground black pepper

basmati rice, popadoms and lime wedges, to serve

SERVES 4

Peeled raw tiger prawns/jumbo shrimp are ideal for this colourful, citrussy curry.

Heat the oil in a large frying pan/skillet. Add the onion, garlic, ginger and chilli/chile and cook for 5 minutes over medium heat.

Add the turmeric, curry powder, ground coriander and cumin and mix well. Transfer to the slow cooker and stir in the tomatoes, stock and lime juice. Cover with the lid and cook on HIGH for 3 hours.

Add the prawns/shrimp and cook for a further 1¼ hours.

Stir in the chopped coriander/cilantro and serve with basmati rice, popadoms and lime wedges.

Mediterranean chunky fish stew with cheese toasts

If you have ever tasted the classic French fish soup bouillabaisse and enjoyed the flavour, then this is a good slow cooker version. The combination of saffron, orange and fennel gives the stew its distinctive flavour. If you can't find Noilly Prat, use dry Martini or a dry white wine in its place.

1 tablespoon olive oil

1 small onion, finely chopped

2 garlic cloves; 1 crushed, 1 halved

a pinch of dried thyme

125 g/4 oz. fennel, cored and finely chopped

50 ml/scant ¼ cup Noilly Prat, dry Martini, or dry white wine

300 ml/1¼ cups passata (Italian sieved tomatoes)

a pinch of saffron threads

freshly squeezed juice and grated zest of 1 orange

200 g/7 oz. skinless cod fillet, cut into large chunks

4 thin slices of baguette

50 g/1 cup finely grated Emmental or Gruyère cheese

sea salt and freshly ground black pepper

SERVES 2

Heat the oil in a large saucepan. Add the onion, crushed garlic, thyme and fennel and gently fry for about 6–8 minutes until soft. Add the Noilly Prat and let bubble, uncovered, until the liquid has almost reduced to nothing.

Add the passata, saffron, orange juice and zest, and 150 ml/⅔ cup cold water. Increase the heat. Add the cod fillet and bring to the boil. Transfer to the slow cooker, season to taste and cook on LOW for 2–2½ hours.

Meanwhile, preheat the grill/broiler to high. Toast the baguette slices on each side under the grill/broiler until lightly golden. Rub the halved garlic over each slice and sprinkle with the grated cheese.

Ladle the stew into warmed deep serving bowls and balance the cheese-topped toasts on top. Serve immediately.

prawn/shrimp & bean rice

This makes a great light dish. The creamy butter/lima beans work surprisingly well with the prawns/shrimp. Feel free to add additional vegetables of your choice. Peas, green beans or sweetcorn/corn kernels all make a good addition, however adding frozen food to a slow cooker isn't recommended, so if using frozen, defrost first.

1 large onion, chopped

1 teaspoon ground turmeric

400-g/14-oz. can chopped tomatoes

1 large red (bell) pepper, seeded and finely chopped

1–2 garlic cloves, chopped

500 ml/2 cups fish or vegetable stock

200 g/1 cup basmati rice

400-g/14-oz. can butter/lima beans, drained and rinsed

1–2 fresh red chillies/chiles, seeded and thinly sliced

500 g/1 lb. 2 oz. cooked peeled prawns/shrimp, defrosted if frozen

3 tablespoons fresh coriander/cilantro, coarsely chopped

sea salt and freshly ground black pepper

SERVES 4

Put the onion, turmeric, tomatoes, (bell) pepper, garlic and stock in the slow cooker. Cover with the lid and cook on HIGH for 3 hours until the vegetables are tender.

Add the rice, butter/lima beans and chillies/chiles and stir through gently. Replace the lid and cook for a further 30 minutes. Stir in the prawns/shrimp, replace the lid and cook for another 10 minutes until the stock is absorbed and the prawns/shrimp are warmed through. Season to taste.

Stir in the coriander/cilantro and serve immediately.

Tip: For a speedier preparation time, pour a jar of prepared marinara sauce, 1 teaspoon ground turmeric, and 500 ml/2 cups fish or vegetable stock into the slow cooker. Cover with the lid and cook on HIGH for 2 hours. Add the rice, butter/lima beans, prawns/shrimp, chilli/chile, seasoning and coriander/cilantro as directed above.

shellfish, tomato & couscous stew

2 tablespoons light olive oil

1 red onion, chopped

1 garlic clove, chopped

1 small red (bell) pepper, seeded and thinly sliced

750 ml/3 cups chicken stock

2 tomatoes, chopped

3 heaped tablespoons couscous

10–12 saffron threads

300 g/10 oz. any firm white fish fillet, cut into bite-size cubes

12 mussels, scrubbed and cleaned of beards

12 raw peeled tiger prawns/jumbo shrimp

4 small squids, hoods cut into 1-cm/ ½-inch wide pieces (optional)

a large handful of chopped fresh parsley

sea salt and freshly ground black pepper

lemon wedges, to serve (optional)

SERVES 4

This is a very simple and tasty summer dish featuring ripe tomatoes with a combination of really fresh seafood. Once you become more familiar with the recipe you can add any combination of your favourite seafood – pieces of salmon fillet (replacing the white fish) would work very well. Couscous shows its versatility in this recipe too, acting as a thickener, like rice, barley or pasta.

Heat the olive oil in a saucepan set over high heat. Add the onion, garlic and (bell) pepper and cook for 4–5 minutes until softened.

Add the stock, tomatoes, couscous and saffron to the pan and bring to the boil. Season lightly. Add the white fish and mussels.

Transfer to the slow cooker. Cover with the lid and cook on LOW for 1½ hours, then add the prawns/shrimp and squid (if using) and cook on LOW for a further 30 minutes. (If using squid do not cook for longer than 30 minutes as overcooking it will make it tough.)

Stir in the parsley, then serve in bowls with lemon wedges on the side to squeeze over, if using.

Moroccan fish stew with mint

900 g/2 lbs. skinless chunky fresh fish fillets, such as cod or haddock, cut into large chunks

2–3 tablespoons olive oil

1 red onion, finely chopped

2 carrots, finely chopped

2 celery stalks, finely chopped

1 preserved lemon, pips discarded and flesh finely chopped

400-g/14-oz. can plum tomatoes

150 ml/⅔ cup fish stock or water

150 ml/⅔ cup white wine or fino sherry

sea salt and freshly ground black pepper

a handful of shredded fresh mint, to garnish

new potatoes and salad greens, to serve (optional)

chermoula

2–3 garlic cloves, chopped

1 fresh red chilli/chile, seeded and chopped

1 teaspoon sea salt

a small bunch of fresh coriander/cilantro, roughly chopped

a pinch of saffron threads

2 teaspoons ground cumin

3–4 tablespoons olive oil

freshly squeezed juice of 1 lemon

SERVES 4–6

The fish stews of coastal Morocco are often made with whole fish, or with large chunks of fleshy fish such as sea bass, monkfish and cod. The fish is first marinated in the classic chermoula flavouring, and this tasty dish is given an additional fillip with a little white wine or sherry. Serve with new potatoes and leafy salad greens, if liked.

First, make the chermoula. Simply whizz all the ingredients together in a blender or small food processor. Reserve about 2 teaspoons of the mixture for cooking. Toss the fish chunks in the remaining chermoula, cover, and let marinate in the fridge for 1–2 hours.

Heat the oil in a frying pan/skillet. Add the onion, carrots and celery and fry for 2–3 minutes until softened. Add the preserved lemon (reserving a little for sprinkling), the reserved 2 teaspoons of chermoula and the tomatoes, and stir in well. Cook gently for about 5 minutes to reduce the liquid slightly, then add the stock and the wine. Bring the liquid to the boil, then transfer to the slow cooker. Stir the marinated fish and marinade into the sauce, cover with the lid and cook on HIGH for 3 hours.

Season to taste, sprinkle with the reserved preserved lemon and the shredded mint leaves, and serve immediately with potatoes and salad greens, if liked.

VEGETARIAN DISHES

potato, basil & green bean risotto

At first you might be alarmed at the combination of potatoes, rice and beans. Don't be, because it's absolutely delicious and makes a substantial meal. Spooning fresh pesto on top before serving is optional, but if you love basil, this will intensify the flavour dramatically.

4 new potatoes, scrubbed and cut into 1-cm/½-inch cubes

50 g/2 oz. green beans, cut into 1-cm/½-inch lengths

800 ml/3¼ cups hot vegetable stock

50 g/3 tablespoons unsalted butter

1 tablespoon olive oil

6–8 shallots, depending on size, finely chopped

2 garlic cloves, crushed

275 g/1½ cups risotto rice, such as arborio

75 ml/⅓ cup white wine

100 g/1½ cups grated vegetarian Italian hard cheese

a large handful of fresh basil, leaves torn

sea salt and freshly ground black pepper

to serve

fresh basil leaves

extra virgin olive oil (optional)

fresh pesto (optional)

SERVES 4

Put the potatoes and beans in the slow cooker with half the hot stock. Cover with the lid and cook on HIGH for 2 hours. About 15 minutes before the end of cooking time, heat the butter and oil in a saucepan set over medium heat. Add the shallots and cook for 1–2 minutes until softened but not browned. Add the garlic and mix well.

Add the rice to the pan and stir, using a wooden spoon, for about 1 minute until the grains are well coated and glistening. Pour in the wine and stir until it has been completely absorbed.

Transfer to the slow cooker and stir into the potato and bean mixture along with the remaining hot stock. Cover with the lid and cook on HIGH for 1 hour. The risotto is ready when the liquid has been absorbed and the rice is tender but still firm (al dente). Turn off the slow cooker, cover with the lid, and let rest for 3–4 minutes.

Add the grated Italian hard cheese and basil and season to taste. Mix well. Spoon into serving bowls, top with basil leaves and drizzle with olive oil or fresh pesto, if using. Serve immediately.

lemon, fennel & mushroom risotto

The lemon adds a delicious lightness of flavour to this unusual risotto. Do use a good risotto rice such as arborio or carnaroli. Beating the risotto at the end of cooking gives this dish its lovely creamy quality. Serve it with plenty of freshly grated Italian hard cheese to sprinkle on top.

2 tablespoons olive oil

50 g/3 tablespoons unsalted butter

1 onion, finely chopped

1 fennel bulb, trimmed and chopped, feathery tops reserved

350 g/1½ cups risotto rice

1.25 litres/5 cups hot vegetable stock

coarsely grated zest and freshly squeezed juice of 1 lemon

1 small fresh or dried bay leaf

a few sprigs of fresh tarragon

250 g/9 oz. button mushrooms, sliced

125 g/½ cup mascarpone cheese

75 g/¾ cup grated vegetarian Italian hard cheese

sea salt and freshly ground black pepper

SERVES 4–5

Put half of the oil and half of the butter in a deep frying pan/skillet or saucepan and heat until melted. Add the onion, fennel and a pinch of salt and cook very gently for about 10 minutes until soft and golden but not browned. Add the rice, stir around in the buttery juices and cook over medium heat for 2–3 minutes until the rice looks translucent.

Transfer to the slow cooker and add about 750 ml/3 cups of the hot stock, ½ teaspoon salt, half of the lemon zest, the bay leaf and tarragon. Mix together, cover with the lid and cook on HIGH for 1 hour, then stir in the remaining stock and cook for a further 25–30 minutes. The risotto is ready when the liquid has been absorbed and the rice is tender but still firm (al dente).

Meanwhile, heat the remaining oil and butter in a frying pan/skillet and cook the mushrooms over medium heat until tender but not browned. Increase the heat and squeeze in half of the lemon juice. Let the liquid evaporate, then take the mushrooms off the heat.

As soon as the rice is cooked, beat in the mascarpone, most of the remaining lemon juice and half the cheese. Stir in the mushrooms and season to taste. Turn off the slow cooker, cover and let rest for 3–4 minutes. Stir well and serve in warmed serving bowls, sprinkled with the chopped fennel tops and the remaining lemon zest. Serve with the remaining cheese.

risotto with cannellini beans

Cannellini beans with pasta or rice make a much-loved meal in Italy. Other beans, such as borlotti or flageolets, are also delicious. Use arborio risotto rice in this dish as it will give a creamy texture.

50 g/3 tablespoons unsalted butter

2 tablespoons olive oil

8 shallots, finely chopped

2 garlic cloves, crushed

275 g/1½ cups risotto rice, such as arborio

75 ml/⅓ cup white wine

900 ml/3⅔ cups hot vegetable stock

250 g/1¼ cups canned cannellini beans, rinsed and drained

4 firm tomatoes, seeded and chopped

finely grated zest of 1 lemon

100 g/1½ cups grated vegetarian Italian hard cheese

a handful of torn fresh basil leaves or finely chopped rosemary

a handful of chopped fresh flat-leaf parsley

sea salt and freshly ground black pepper

extra virgin olive oil, to serve (optional)

SERVES 4

Heat the butter and 1 tablespoon of the oil in a sauté pan set over medium heat. Add the shallots and cook for 1–2 minutes, until softened but not browned. Add the garlic and mix well.

Add the rice and stir, using a wooden spoon, for about 1 minute, until the grains are well coated and glistening. Pour in the wine and stir until it has been completely absorbed.

Add 1 ladle of hot stock and simmer, stirring until it has been absorbed. After 10 minutes, add the cannellini beans, tomatoes and lemon zest and mix well. Transfer the ingredients to the slow cooker and add more hot stock to make up to 700 ml/2¾ cups altogether. Cover with the lid and cook on HIGH for 1 hour.

After 1 hour, stir well, add the remaining hot stock, replace the lid and cook for a further 30 minutes. The risotto is ready when the liquid has been absorbed and the rice is tender but still firm (al dente). Turn off the slow cooker, cover and let rest for 3–4 minutes.

Add the cheese and half of the herbs and season to taste. Spoon into warmed serving bowls, sprinkle with the remaining herbs and drizzle with olive oil, if using. Serve immediately.

smoky bean hotpot

This is a hearty and filling bean hotpot packed with vegetables and rich with smoky Spanish paprika.

2 tablespoons olive oil

1 large onion, chopped

2 garlic cloves, chopped

1 tablespoon capers, finely chopped

3 tablespoons chopped fresh flat-leaf parsley

2 teaspoons smoked sweet Spanish paprika (pimentón dulce)

1 celery stalk, chopped

1 carrot, chopped

2 medium waxy potatoes, cut into 2.5-cm/1-inch dice

1 red (bell) pepper, seeded and chopped

350 ml/1½ cups hot vegetable stock

400-g/14-oz. can butter/lima beans

sea salt and freshly ground black pepper

crusty bread, to serve

SERVES 4

Put the oil in a saucepan set over medium heat. Add the onion and cook for 4–5 minutes until softened. Add the garlic, capers, parsley and paprika to the pan and stir-fry for 2 minutes.

Add the celery, carrot, potatoes and red (bell) pepper and cook for 2 minutes, stirring constantly to coat the vegetables in the flavoured oil. Transfer to the slow cooker and add the stock.

Cover with the lid and cook on HIGH for 3 hours until all the vegetables are cooked. Stir in the butter/lima beans 1 hour before the end of cooking time.

Season to taste and serve with crusty bread.

mushroom & thyme ragù
with hand-torn pasta

Many exotic mushroom varieties are now cultivated and can be bought year-round, offering a constant supply of just about any mushroom you could wish for. A mixture has been used here, including meaty field mushrooms as they go hand in hand with the other comforting, rich flavours of fresh thyme, red wine and cinnamon.

2 tablespoons olive oil

2 tablespoons unsalted butter

1 onion, chopped

2 garlic cloves, chopped

3 portobello mushrooms, caps removed and cut into 2.5-cm/1-inch pieces

200 g/7 oz. button mushrooms

100 g/3½ oz. shiitake mushrooms, quartered

3 fresh thyme sprigs

200 ml/¾ cup red wine

1 cinnamon stick

100 ml/scant ½ cup vegetable stock

400 g/14 oz. fresh lasagne sheets, torn into thick strips

sea salt and freshly ground black pepper

grated vegetarian Italian hard cheese, to serve

SERVES 4

Heat the oil and butter in a heavy-based saucepan set over medium heat. Add the onion and garlic and cook for 4–5 minutes until the onion has softened.

Increase the heat, add the mushrooms and thyme and cook for a further 8–10 minutes, stirring often, until the mushrooms darken and soften.

Add the red wine and cinnamon to the pan and boil for 5 minutes. Pour in the stock and season well. Transfer everything to the slow cooker, cover with the lid and cook on HIGH for 2 hours.

Cook the pasta in a saucepan of boiling water for 2–3 minutes, until it rises to the surface. Drain well and put in warmed serving bowls. Spoon the mushroom ragù on top and sprinkle with grated Italian hard cheese to serve.

three-cheese macaroni

*Macaroni cheese is a firm comfort food favourite. Here it's given
a modern makeover with mascarpone, Cheddar, Italian hard cheese
and a touch of garlic. If you like a crisp topping, you can simply pop
the slow cooker dish under a preheated grill/broiler to brown for a few
minutes before serving.*

2 tablespoons butter

1 garlic clove, finely chopped

1 teaspoon dry mustard powder

3 tablespoons plain/all-purpose flour

600 ml/2⅓ cups milk

125 ml/½ cup mascarpone cheese

130 g/1 cup grated mature/sharp
Cheddar cheese

60 g/½ cup grated vegetarian Italian
hard cheese

250 g/9 oz. dried tube pasta, such as
macaroni, penne or rigatoni

toasted breadcrumbs, to serve

sea salt and freshly ground
black pepper

SERVES 4

Melt the butter in a medium saucepan and use some to brush the
inside of the slow cooker dish. Add the garlic and mustard to the
pan and fry for 1 minute before adding the flour. Whisk constantly
over medium heat until it forms a paste. Gradually whisk in the
milk and increase the heat. Bring to the boil, whisking constantly.
Remove from the heat and stir in the mascarpone, Cheddar and
half of the Italian hard cheese.

Boil the pasta in plenty of salted water until just al dente. Drain
and mix with the cheese sauce. Season to taste and spoon the
mixture into the slow cooker. Top with the remaining Italian hard
cheese. Cover with the lid and cook on LOW for 2–3 hours.

Sprinkle with the toasted breadcrumbs to serve.

winter vegetable tagine

3 tablespoons olive oil

1 onion, chopped

2 garlic cloves, chopped

½ teaspoon ground turmeric

½ teaspoon paprika

1 teaspoon ground cumin

1 cinnamon stick

300 ml/1¼ cups vegetable stock

400-g/14-oz. can chopped tomatoes

1 large carrot, peeled and cut into
thick batons

1 parsnip, peeled and cut into 2.5-cm/
1-inch pieces

1 turnip, peeled and cut into 1-cm/
½-inch thick rounds

125 g/4 oz. sweet potato, peeled and
cut into cubes

1 green apple, peeled, cored and cut
into 8 wedges

a small handful of chopped fresh mint

sea salt and freshly ground
black pepper

couscous or rice, to serve

SERVES 4

*Although it sounds rather exotic, a tagine is really
nothing more complicated than a stew. It really can have
just about anything you like in it, provided there are the
obligatory fragrant and aromatic spices, so typical of
Moroccan cooking. It's these heavy, pungent spices that
work so well here with full-flavoured winter vegetables.*

Heat the oil in a heavy-based saucepan. Add the onion and garlic
and cook over high heat for 2–3 minutes. Add all of the spices and
cook for 2 minutes more until aromatic but not burning.

Add the stock and the tomatoes and season well. Bring to the
boil and add the carrot, parsnip, turnip, sweet potato and apple.
Transfer to the slow cooker, cover with the lid, and cook on HIGH
for 3 hours.

Stir in the mint then spoon the vegetables over couscous or rice
to serve.

root vegetable ragù

3 tablespoons olive oil

2 tablespoons unsalted butter

1 red onion, chopped

1 celery stalk, roughly chopped

6 garlic cloves, lightly smashed

250 ml/1 cup passata (Italian sieved tomatoes)

250 ml/1 cup vegetable stock

2 tablespoons fresh oregano leaves or 1 teaspoon dried oregano

1 parsnip, chopped

2 carrots, chopped

6 small, waxy, new potatoes, chopped

sea salt and freshly ground black pepper

couscous or rice, to serve

SERVES 4

This is a hearty dish packed with nutritious root vegetables – perfect comfort food for vegetarians.

Put the oil and butter in a large frying pan/skillet set over medium heat. When the butter sizzles, add the onion, celery and garlic. Cook for 1–2 minutes, then add the remaining ingredients, season to taste and bring to the boil.

Transfer to the slow cooker, cover with the lid and cook on HIGH for 2–3 hours until the vegetables are tender.

Spoon the ragù over couscous or rice to serve.

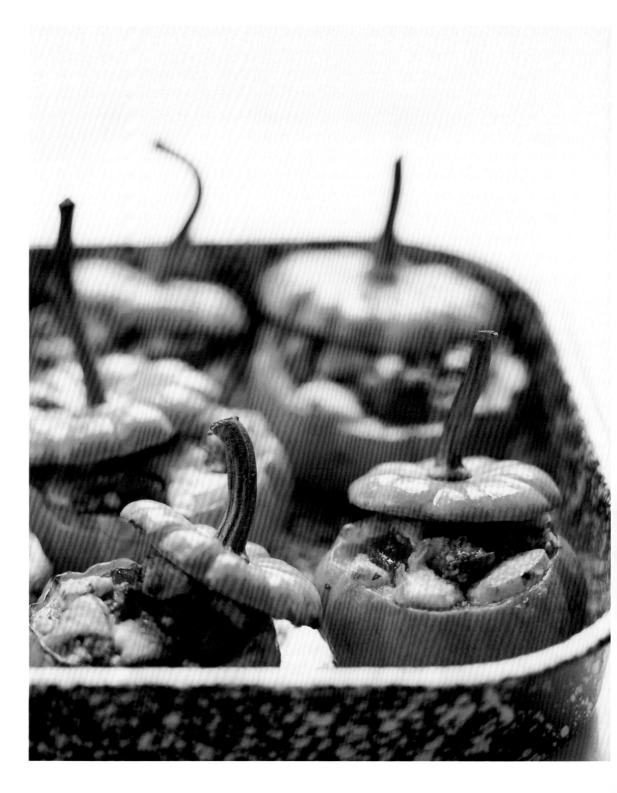

stuffed squash with pesto & mozzarella

Choose small sugar pumpkins or butternut squash for this recipe. This colourful dish is marvellous served with crisp salad leaves as a vegetarian main course.

2 small butternut squash or 4 sugar pumpkins, washed and dried

1 tablespoon olive oil, plus extra to drizzle

½ small red onion, chopped

1 garlic clove, crushed

8 cherry tomatoes, halved

a large handful of fresh basil leaves

2 tablespoons fresh vegetarian pesto

75 g/2½ oz. mozzarella cheese, torn into pieces

sea salt and freshly ground black pepper

crisp, peppery salad greens, to serve (optional)

SERVES 2

If using butternut squash, cut them just as they start to narrow into a waist and scoop out the seeds. You're aiming for a hollow receptacle. (Save the butternut squash tops for another recipe. However, if using sugar pumpkins or small squash, simply slice off the tops and reserve these for decoration.)

Arrange the squash in the base of the slow cooker, trimming off any end parts to make them fit if slightly too big.

Heat the oil in a frying pan/skillet, add the onion and garlic and fry for 2–3 minutes until softened. Remove from the heat and stir in the tomatoes, basil, pesto and mozzarella. Season well then divide the filling between the squash. Drizzle a little olive oil over the top and then very carefully pour in enough water to come just under halfway up the sides of the squash. You do not want to spill any water on or in the squash or to allow the filling of the squash to come into contact with the water.

Cover with the lid and cook on HIGH for 3 hours until the squash is tender.

Serve hot with crisp, peppery salad greens, if liked.

ratatouille

Ratatouille is simply the best all-purpose vegetable dish there is. It goes perfectly with any main dish or served with rice or crusty bread for a vegetarian meal. It also makes a great filling for a savoury pancake when sprinkled with cheese and finished off under the grill/broiler.

3 tablespoons olive oil

1 onion, finely sliced

3 garlic cloves, crushed

a handful of chopped fresh flat-leaf parsley

1 large aubergine/eggplant, cubed

2–3 red and/or yellow (bell) peppers, seeded and cubed

4 medium courgette/zucchini, sliced

¼ teaspoon sea salt

400-g/14-oz. can chopped tomatoes

2 teaspoons red wine vinegar or balsamic vinegar

sea salt and freshly ground black pepper

rice or crusty bread, to serve

SERVES 6

Heat the oil in a large, heavy-based saucepan set over medium heat. Add the onion, garlic and flat-leaf parsley and fry for 10 minutes, stirring regularly.

Add the aubergine/eggplant and cook for 5 minutes. Add the (bell) peppers and courgettes/zucchini and stir in the salt. Cook for a few minutes, then add the chopped tomatoes.

Transfer to the slow cooker, cover with the lid, and cook on HIGH for 3½ hours. About 1 hour before the end of the cooking time, stir in the vinegar and season to taste.

Serve warm with rice or bread.

index

recipe credits

Sonia Stevenson
chicken and sweet potatoes with honey, soy and lemon
chicken tagine with quinces and preserved lemons
Greek braised lamb with okra
Irish carbonnade
Lancashire hotpot
Provençal daube of beef
slow cooker stock
Tuscan pork and bean casserole
Vietnamese beef
Yankee pot roast

Ross Dobson
garlic and chilli rice soup with spring greens
lamb kefta meatballs
mushroom and thyme ragù with hand-torn pasta
root vegetable ragù with spiced couscous
Scotch broth
shellfish, tomato and couscous stew
smoky bean hotpot
winter vegetable tagine

Fran Warde
beef and carrot casserole with cheese dumplings
chicken and bacon pot
chicken soup
chili con carne
classic minestrone
eggs cocotte
golden butternut squash soup
meatloaf with tomato sauce
prawn curry

Laura Washburn
braised pork chops with tomato, orange, and chilli
chicken, sausage and rice
meatballs in red pepper sauce
Portuguese lamb stew with piri piri

Fiona Smith
beef and ale pâté
blue cheese fondue
pork, fennel and spinach terrine
ratatouille

Fiona Beckett
coq au vin
duck casserole with red wine, cinnamon and olives
lamb shanks with red wine, rosemary and garlic

Maxine Clark
Mexican pork and beans in red chilli sauce
smoked and fresh salmon terrine
spinach and ricotta timbales

Silvana Franco
Italian pasta and bean soup
pancetta and turkey meatballs
rich Bolognese sauce

Brian Glover
lemon, fennel and mushroom risotto

Rachael Anne Hill
bag-cooked chicken with runner beans
chicken and barley braise
prawn and butter bean rice

Sunil Vijayakar
beef and pea curry
beef madras
butter chicken
lamb rogan josh

Liz Franklin
lamb and butternut squash stew
tagliatelle with rich meat sauce

Manisha Gambhir Harkins
Burmese pork hinleh
red-cooked chicken legs

Tonia George
chicken and lentil curry
lamb and broad bean tagine

Jennifer Joyce
three-cheese macaroni

Caroline Marson
chicken jalfrezi
Spanish sausage and butter bean casserole

Elsa Petersen-Schepelern
spicy chicken curry with butternut and spinach
stuffed squash with pesto and mozzarella

Ursula Ferrigno
potato, basil and green bean risotto
risotto with cannellini beans

Ghillie Basan
Moroccan fish stew

Jane Milton (Not Just Food Ltd)
slow cooker know-how (introduction)

picture credits

Page 6: Image courtesy of Cuisinart: Cuisinart Cook & Hold slow cooker. Call Cuisinart on 1-800-211-9604 or visit www.cuisinart.com for further information.

Page 7: Image courtesy of Crock-Pot®—the original slow cooker brand. Visit www.crockpot.com for further information.

Caroline Arber
Pages 14, 21, 26, 41, 47, 48, 86, 92, 96,126

Martin Brigdale
Pages 11, 69, 90, 134, 149, 157

Peter Cassidy
Page 2, 37, 38, 61, 79, 91, 94, 102, 108, 109, 115, 124, 128, 156

Nicki Dowey
Pages 1, 119, 120, 130

Tara Fisher
Pages 40

Richard Jung
Pages 18, 20, 22, 25, 27, 70, 122, 133, 136, 141, 144, 146, 147, 150, 153

William Lingwood
Page 8, 10, 11, 17, 28, 39, 33, 34, 42, 44, 51, 52, 55, 56, 59, 60, 80, 84, 98, 100, 103, 112, 116, 151

Jason Lowe
Pages, 139, 142

David Munns
Pages 4, 63, 64, 67, 68, 111, 148

Noel Murphy
Pages 88

William Reavell
Page 12, 76, 106

Yuki Sugiura
Pages 5, 19

Debi Treloar
Pages 85, 123, 154

Pia Tryde
Page 57

Ian Wallace
Page 29

Kate Whitaker
Pages 71, 72, 75, 83, 104, 127